Narratology

JANUA
LINGUARUM Series Maior 108

Studia Memoriae
Nicolai van Wijk Dedicata

edenda curat

C. H. van Schooneveld

Indiana University

P
302
.P75
1982

Narratology

The Form and Functioning of Narrative

Gerald Prince

WITHDRAWN

Mouton Publishers
Berlin · New York · Amsterdam

HIEBERT LIBRARY
Fresno Pacific College - M. B. Seminary
Fresno, Calif 93702   60470

Library of Congress Cataloging in Publication Data

Prince, Gerald.
   Narratology: the form and funtioning of
narrative.

   (Janua Linguarum. Series Maior; 108)
   Bibliography: p.
   Includes index.
   1. Discourse analysis, Narrative. I. Title.
II. Series.
P302. P75   808.3'00141   82-6415
ISBN 90-279-3090-2   AACR2

ISBN 90 279 3090 2

© Copyright 1982 by Walter de Gruyter & Co., Berlin. All rights reserved, including those of translation into foreign languages. No part of this book may be reproduced in any form – by photoprint, microfilm, or any other means – nor transmitted nor translated into a machine language without written permission from the publisher. Typesetting: Grestun Graphics, Abingdon. – Printing: Druckerei Hildebrand, Berlin. – Binding: Lüderitz & Bauer Buchgewerbe GmbH. Printed in Germany.

Contents

Introduction

In his " An Introduction to the Structural Analysis of Narrative,"
Roland Barthes writes:

There are countless forms of narrative in the world. First of all, there is a
prodigious variety of genres, each of which branches out into a variety of
media, as if all substances could be relied upon to accommodate man's stories.
Among the vehicles of narrative are articulated language, whether oral or
written, pictures, still or moving, gestures, and an ordered mixture of all these
substances; narrative is present in myth, legend, fables, tales, short stories,
epics, history, tragedy, *drame* [suspense drama], comedy, pantomime, paint-
ings (in Santa Ursula by Carpaccio, for instance), stained-glass windows,
movies, local news, conversation. Moreover, in this infinite variety of forms, it
is present at all times, in all places, in all societies; indeed narrative starts with
the very history of mankind; there is not, there has never been anywhere, any
people without narrative; all classes, all human groups have their stories, and
very often those stories are enjoyed by men of different and even opposite
cultural backgrounds: narrative remains largely unconcerned with good
or bad literature. Like life itself, it is there, international, transhistorical,
transcultural.[1]

Narrative, indeed universal and infinitely varied, may be defined
as the representation of real or fictive events and situations in a
time sequence.

Note that, although many — not to say all — representations can
be said to be linked to the dimension of time, not all of them constitute narratives. In

(1)   Roses are red/ Violets are blue/ Sugar is sweet/ And so
      are you,

(2)   Roses are red

could be said to come in time before

(3)   Violets are blue

However, this temporal dimension has nothing whatever to do with the objects or events represented; rather, it has to do with (the production or reception of) their representation. In the world represented, roses are not red **before** violets are blue and violets are not blue **before** sugar is sweet. With narratives, on the other hand, we can speak of temporal sequence not only at the representational level but also at the repesented one. In the world referred to by

(4)   John was very rich then he began to gamble and he became very poor

John's being very rich does precede in time his being very poor.

Note also that, although many things (not to say anything) take time, at least some of their representations do not necessarily constitute a narrative. A fight can take a few minutes and a trip can take a few hours yet neither

(5)   There was a fight yesterday

nor

(6)   It was a beautiful trip

constitute narratives: they do not represent the fight nor the trip as a series of events but as one event.

According to our definition, some messages — however trivial — clearly qualify as narrative while others — however interesting — do not. For example, (4),

(7)   Mary drank a glass of orange juice then she drank a glass of milk

and

(8)   A people on the Columbia had no eyes or mouth. They ate by smelling the sturgeon. Coyote gave them eyes and a mouth

as well as *Les Trois Mousquetaires, The Secret Agent,* or *The Peloponnesian War* satisfy the definition and, in fact, would generally be considered narrative. On the other hand, (1),

(9)   All men are mortal; Socrates is a man; Socrates is mortal
and
(10)   It is 90° in New York and it is 95° in Philadelphia

as well as *Language, Truth and Logic* and *Tractatus Logico-Philosophicus* do not satisfy the definition and, in fact, would generally not be considered narrative. But what about simple statements like

(11)   John got out of the room
or
(12)   Bill opened the door

which could be claimed to satisfy the definition? Both (11) and (12) refer us to a series of situations and events in a time sequence: after all, (11) can be restated as

(13)   John was in the room, then he got out of the room, then he was not in the room
and (12) can be restated as
(14)   The door was closed, then Bill opened the door, then, as a result, the door was open

Since (13) and (14) clearly satisfy the definition (in the world represented, John is in the room **before** he gets out of it; the door is closed **before** Bill opens it), (11) and (12) do too and so would many statements describing a simple action. Yet, surely, there is a difference between such statements and narratives. It cannot merely be a difference in significance since (7), for instance, is not much more significant than (11) or (12), if at all. Likewise, it is not enough to say that (11) and (12) each describe explicitly one and only one event, since there are statements which describe a single event and which are sometimes regarded as narratives. In fact, a statement like

(15)   At 2 a.m. yesterday, the U.S. declared war on England

could even be called a news *story*. The difference lies somewhere else. In (11)–(14), two of the three events and situations evoked are presupposed or entailed by the third. Specifically,

(16)   John was in the room

and

(17)   John was not in the room

are presupposed or entailed by (11); and

(18)   The door was closed

and

(19)   The door was open

are presupposed or entailed by (12).[2] Such is not at all the case with (7). Nor is it the case with (15): the latter functions as a story if something like the following reconstruction is made:

(20)   Most people thought that the U.S. would never declare war on England; then, at 2 a.m. yesterday, the U.S. declared war on England; then, as a result, most people were extremely surprised

and it is clear that the reconstructed passages are not necessarily presupposed or entailed by (15).[3]

A redefinition of narrative, taking the preceding into account is called for: narrative is the representation of **at least two** real or fictive events or situations in a time sequence, neither of which presupposes or entails the other.

Narratology is the study of the form and functioning of narrative. Although the term is relatively new, the discipline is not and, in the Western tradition, it goes back at least to Plato and Aristotle. During the twentieth century, narratology has been considerably developed. The last ten or fifteen years, in particular, have witnessed a remarkable growth of narratological activity. The discipline has attracted numerous literary analysts and many linguists, as well as philosophers, psychologists, psychoanalysts, biblicists, semioticians, folklorists, anthropologists, and communication theorists in many parts of the world: Denmark (the 'Copenhagen Group'), France (Barthes, Bremond, Genette, Greimas, Hamon, Kristeva, Todorov, etc.) Germany (Ihwe, Schmidt, etc.), Italy (Eco, Segre), the Netherlands (van Dijk), North America (Chatman, Colby, Doležel, Dundes, Georges, Hendricks, Labov, Pavel, Scholes, etc.), the U.S.S.R. (Lotman, Toporov, Uspenski, etc.).

Narratology examines what all narratives have in common —

narratively speaking – and what allows them to be narratively different. It is therefore not so much concerned with the history of particular novels or tales, or with their meaning, or with their esthetic value, but rather with the traits which distinguish narrative from other signifying systems and with the modalities of these traits. Its corpus consists not only of all extant narratives, but of all possible ones. As for its primary task, it is the elaboration of instruments leading to the explicit description of narratives and the comprehension of their functioning.

I attempt in this study to answer three questions of central concern to narratologists: what are the features of narrative which allow us to characterize its possible manifestations in pertinent terms (Chapters one and two)? what would a formal model accounting for these features and manifestations look like (Chapter three)? what are the factors which affect our understanding of a narrative and our evaluation of its narrativity (Chapters four and five)?

In my presentation, I focus on written narrative because it is the kind I know best. However, much of what I say is applicable to any narrative regardless of the medium of representation. I do not try to discuss everything that is known about narrative nor even everything that should be known; but, at the risk of frequently stating the obvious and of repeating even more frequently what others have said very well before me (my debt to Roland Barthes, Wayne C. Booth, Gérard Genette, Tzvetan Todorov, and many more is clearly tremendous), I try to discuss, however briefly, most of what I think must be known. For the sake of convenience, clarity and brevity, and to emphasize the fact that the domain of narratology consists of all narratives and not merely great ones, or literary ones, or interesting ones, I often use as examples (parts of) narratives of which I am the author. Finally, many of the translations are my own. I hope that it will not be too obvious.

Some of the material in this book has already appeared in *Centrum* I(1) (1973), *Poétique* (14) (1973), *Poetics Today* I(3) (1980) and my *A Grammar of Stories: An Introduction*, published by Mouton and Co. I should like to thank the editors and publishers for permission to reprint.

I should also like to thank Ellen F. Prince for many stimulating discussions.

CHAPTER ONE

Narrating

A narrative is, among other things, a collection of signs which can be grouped into various classes. More particularly, in written narrative, certain features and combinations of the linguistic signs making up the narrative constitute **signs of the narrating** (or **narrating**, for short): they represent the narrating activity, its origin and its destination. Other features and combinations constitute **signs of the narrated** (or **narrated** for short): they represent the events and situations recounted. Each of these two classes may in turn be divided into sub-classes. Thus, among signs of the narrating some pertain more specifically to the narrator (the one who narrates), others to his narratee (the one who is narrated to) and others still to his narration (the act of his narrating); and among signs of the narrated, some pertain more specifically to characters, for instance, others to the time during which the characters act, and others still to the space in which their actions occur.

THE NARRATOR

In grammar, a distinction is made among the first person ('I', for example), the second person ('you') and the third person ('he'). The first person is defined as the one who speaks, the second person as the one who is spoken to, and the third person as the being or object that is spoken about. Similar distinctions can be made in narratology: we can say that the narrator is a first person, the narratee a second person and the being or object narrated about a third person.

In a given sentence, an 'I' representing the speaker may or may not appear, of course. Consider my saying the following:

(1)   I am a plumber
(2)   Paris is the capital of France
(3)   Mary took her exams in July.

Similarly, in a given narrative, an 'I' representing the narrator may or may not appear. Consider my narrating the following:

(4)   I go to the refrigerator, take out a can of beer and drink it.
(5)   He goes to the refrigerator, takes out a can of beer and drinks it
(6)   Joan is rich. She meets John and she becomes very poor.

There is at least one narrator in any narrative and this narrator may or may not be explicitly designated by an 'I'. In many narratives where he is not, the 'I' may have been deleted without leaving any traces but the narrative itself: there is nothing in (5) and (6) which refers to or implies a narrating activity and, therefore, a narrating self except for the fact that they are narratives. In many narratives where he is, the 'I' may constitute the only reference to his narrating self. Thus, in (4), we learn nothing explicit about the narrator as such, except that he is recounting events in which he takes part: we do not know what he thinks of these events as he is narrating them; we do not perceive what his attitude towards his narration is; and so on and so forth. Although he describes his own actions, (4) is not really more subjective than (5) or (6). Indeed, in (4), (5), and (6) respectively, 'I', 'he', and 'Joan' do not function in a significantly different fashion: they each act simply as a character's name. But there are also many narratives where numerous signs representing the narrator and signifying his presence in the narrative are evident, whether or not an 'I' designating him ever appears.

1.   Signs of the 'I'

Some of these signs may function indirectly. Thus, any second person pronoun which does not (exclusively) refer to a character and is not uttered (or "thought") by him must refer to someone whom a narrator is addressing and therefore constitutes a trace of the latter's presence in the narrative. Consider for example,

(7) "All is true, – so true that you may recognize its elements in your experience, and even find its seeds within your soul" (*Le Père Goriot*),

and

(8) As you know, John went to France then he went to Germany.

But some – we can call them signs of the 'I' – function more directly and represent the narrator and/or his spatio-temporal situation.[1] It is clear, for instance, that any first person plural pronoun which does not exclusively designate characters (or narratees) refers to a narrating self:

(9) "We will confess that, following the example of many a serious author, we have started our hero's story one year before his birth" (*La Chartreuse de Parme*)

(10) "To sum up the points to which we have directed attention, three kinds of ravages nowadays disfigure Gothic architecture" (*Notre-Dame de Paris*)

Furthermore, there is a class of deictic terms ('now', 'here', 'yesterday', 'tomorrow', and so on) which relate to the situation of their utterance and, more particularly, to the spatio-temporal situation of the utterer. Should one of them appear in a narrative and should it not be part of a character's utterance, it must be related to a narrator. In

(11) Mary went to the beach yesterday, then she went to the movies, then she went home,

(12) "Then, some sixty years ago, a sudden change took place. The gin-pits were elbowed aside by the large mines of the financiers" (*Sons and Lovers*)

and

(13) John came here, he got drunk and he left,

'yesterday', 'some sixty years ago' and 'here' characterize the narrator's spatio-temporal situation. There is also a class of modal terms ('perhaps', 'unfortunately', 'clearly', and so forth) which indicate a speaker's attitude about what he says. Once again, should one of them not be part of a character's utterance, it describes the narrator's position: 'perhaps' and 'clearly' in

> (14)   John went to the movies. Perhaps he was lonely

and

> (15)   John reacted very coldly. Clearly, this was the result of his having suffered too much and too often

function as signs of 'I'. More generally, any sign in a narration which represents a narrator's persona, his attitude, his knowledge of worlds other than that of the narrated, or his interpretation of the events recounted and evaluation of their importance constitutes a sign of the 'I'. Consider the following underlined passages, for example:

> (16)   **People are remarkable.** John was poor and sick; he kept on trying to improve his lot and managed to become rich and healthy
> (17)   He was wearing **one of those flashy ties often seen on Broadway**
> (18)   **Like all people of good taste**, he drove a Cadillac
> (19)   **He must have been scared** since he was sweating profusely.[2]

2.   Intrusiveness, Self-Consciousness, Reliability, Distance

Whether or not the narrator is designated by an 'I', he may therefore be more or less intrusive, that is, more or less explicitly characterized as a narrating self. If we eliminated every narrator's intrusion from *Le Père Goriot*, *Eugénie Grandet* or *Malone meurt*, we would be left with relatively little; but if we did the same with "The Killers", "Hills like White Elephants" or *L'Age de raison*, we would have, relatively, quite a lot to read. Compare

> (20)   "No part of Paris is so depressing, nor we may add, so little known. The Rue Neuve Sainte-Geneviève, above all, may be likened to an iron frame — the only frame fit to hold the coming narrative, to which the reader's mind

must be led by sombre colors and solemn thoughts" (*Le Père Goriot*)

and

(21)   "Outside the arc-light shone through the bare branches of a tree. Nick walked up the street beside the car-tracks and turned at the next arc-light down a side-street. Three houses up the street was Hirsch's rooming house. Nick walked up the two steps and pushed the bell. A woman came to the door." ("The Killers")

Furthermore, intrusions may have different degrees of obviousness. Given a narrative recounting events which took place in Corsica in 1769, for example, 'Emperor' would constitute an intrusion in

(22)   Emperor Napoleon's birth was greeted with joy

since nobody in the world of the narrated could know the newborn baby's destiny. On the other hand, some intrusions are far more evident. In *Tom Jones* the narrator even warns his narratee of the many digressions to come:

(23)   "Reader, I think proper, before we proceed any farther together, to acquaint thee that I intend to digress through this whole history, as often as I see occasion, of which I am myself a better judge than any pitiful critic whatever; and here I must desire all those critics to mind their own business. . . ."

Note that some narratologists would consider the slightest "evaluative" adjective or adverb or the most discreet logical connection between events to be intrusions.[3] Given

(24)   John walked elegantly

and

(25)   Bill was happy because he had just seen Robert

for example, they would regard 'elegantly' and 'because' as intrusive elements. Yet this is not a very convincing position; for there is nothing in (24) and (25) which indicates that perhaps John did not walk elegantly and perhaps Bill's happiness was not the result of his having seen Robert; that is, there is nothing which indicates that the evaluation and the logical connection are the result of the narrator's interpretation, the consequence of his special knowledge, the mere product of his subjectivity rather than well-established facts in the world of the narrated. Indeed, the elegance of John's walk and the cause of Bill's happiness are given as incontrovertible and we take them as such when we read.

If a narrator may be more or less intrusive, he may also be more or less self-conscious, that is, he may seem more or less aware that he is narrating: Jacques Revel in *L'Emploi du temps* — who often discusses the circumstances of his writing — is a self-conscious narrator ("The day before yesterday, as I set down my recollections of the seven-months past Sunday". "That is why I now feel compelled to interrupt the pattern I had been following for the past month in my narrative", "I have used the last inch of daylight to finish rereading my account of the second week in June, written two months ago at this very table") whereas Meursault in *L'Etranger* is not: not once does he comment on the fact that he is telling his own story. Note that, whereas a self-conscious narrator is always intrusive, the reverse is not true: the narrators of (17), (18) and (19) are intrusive without being self-conscious in the least.

A narrator may also be more or less reliable; in other words, (parts of) his account may be more or less worthy of trust in terms of the narrative itself. When reading *La Chute*, we are led to conclude that Jean-Baptiste Clamence is quite unreliable: he is a confirmed liar; he constantly and systematically contradicts himself; and it becomes clear that most of what he says — if not everything — is not supposed to be taken at face value. In *Le Père Goriot*, on the other hand, we are not made to question the narrator's reliablility: no reason is given us — insofar as the fictional world is concerned — for doubting the validity of his account and of his judgments. Note that a reliable narrator is not necessarily one that I — as a reader — always agree with: after all, however honest and trustworthy he may be portrayed as, I may find his values repugnant and his conclusions stupid. Conversely, I may find the attitudes of an unreliable narrator very attractive indeed.

Finally, a narrator may be at a greater or lesser distance from the events narrated, from the characters presented and/or from his narratee. The distance may be temporal (I narrate events which happened yesterday or fifty years ago); it may by physical (Oskar in *The Tin Drum* does not address dwarves); it may be intellectual (the narrator of *The Sound of the Fury* is certainly more intelligent than Benjy), moral (Sade's Justine is far more virtuous than the characters populating her story), emotional (the narrator of "Un Coeur simple" is not as moved as Felicité by Virginie's death), and so forth. Of course, a given distance may vary in the course of a given narrative: at the end of *Great Expectations*, the narrator is temporally closer to the narrated than at the beginning; and in *La Chute* Jean-Baptiste Clamence's narratee resists him more and more as the novel progresses.

The intrusiveness of a given narrator, his degree of self-conscious-ness, his reliability, his distance from the narrated or the narratee not only help characterize him but also affect our interpretation of and response to the narrative. Thus, intrusions commenting on some of the events recounted may bring out or underline their importance in a certain narrated sequence or their intrinsic interest; they may also delight us (if we find them witty, for instance) or annoy us (if we find them superfluous). Intrusions referring to the narrator or the quality of his narration may lead us to conclude that the real subject of the narrative is the rendering of certain events rather than the events themselves and that the real hero is the narrator rather than any one of his characters. Similarly, the narrator's unreliability forces us to reinterpret many of his statements in order to arrive at a knowledge and understanding of "what really happened"; and variations in distance may entail variations in our intellectual appreciation of and emotional commitment to one character or another.[4]

3. Narrator-Character

Just as he may or may not be explicitly designated by an 'I' and whether or not he is intrusive, self-conscious or reliable, the narrator may or may not be a participant in the events he recounts. When he is, we usually speak of a first-person narrative because the first person narrates — among other things — events in which he takes part (*Moll Flanders, Great Expectations, The Great Gatsby*).

We can then make a distinction between the first person as narrator and the first person as character. In

(26)   I ate meat

the character 'I' is the one who ate and the narrator 'I' is the one who tells about the eating; similarly in *Great Expectations*, the mature Pip, who recounts the adventures of his younger self, is different from that younger self; and in *All the King's Men*, the Jack Burden who narrates his own story as well as Willie Stark's is not quite like the Jack Burden who studied history in graduate school, had a couple of nervous breakdowns and worked for Willie. When the narrator is not a character, we usually speak of a third-person narrative, because the events narrated refer to third persons (*Barchester Towers, The Portrait of a Lady, L'Education sentimentale*). Sometimes, of course, the narrator may be a character yet refer to himself as to a third person – as to one character among many others – more or less frequently and systematically. In Thackeray's *Henry Esmond* the protagonist tells his own story mostly in the third person ("'Tis needless in these memoirs to go at any length into the particulars of Harry Esmond's college career"; "Esmond went away only too glad to be the bearer of such good news"; "With the exception of that one cruel letter which he had from his mistress, Mr. Esmond heard nothing from her"); and in Camus' *La Peste*, Dr, Rieux refers to himself as Dr. Rieux through most of the novel. Another possibility – and a relatively seldom exploited one in fiction – is the second-person narrative, where the events narrated pertain to a second person:

(27)   You were both standing in the doorway between the bright room and the dark room, and she was whispering these words not in your ear but against your mouth, with her lips touching yours from time to time (*La Modification*)

(28)   "Sometimes, you stay three, four, five days in your room, you don't know. You sleep almost continuously, you wash your socks, your two shirts. You reread a mystery novel you've already read twenty times, forgotten twenty times" (*Un Homme qui dort*)

Again, the narrator may be a character yet refer to himself as 'you', and in a work like *La Modification* it is difficult — initially, at least — to tell whether the 'you' who is the protagonist designates a narrator-character or not.

In cases where the narrator is a character, he may play a more or less considerable role in the events which he recounts. He may be the protagonist (*The Confessions of Zeno, Great Expectations, Voyage au bout de la nuit, Kiss me deadly*), or an important character (*All the King's Men, La Porte Etroite*), or a minor one (*A Study in Scarlet*), or even a mere observer ("A Rose for Emily"). Sometimes, he may be a character in one part of his narrative but not in another (the 'I' in "Sarrasine") and sometimes, though he plays no part in the events which he himself narrates, he may be a character in events recounted by another narrator (Scheherazade in *Arabian Nights*).

4. Multiple Narrators

Up to now, I have mainly proceeded as though there were only one narrator per narrative and, obviously, this is often the case. Consider (29) or (30), for example, in which one and only one "I" recounts a series of events:

> (29) I was very happy, then I met Peter, then, as a result, I was very unhappy
> (30) Peter was very unhappy, then he met Jane, then, as a result, he was very happy

But there are many narratives with more than one narrator; indeed, in a given narrative, there may be an indefinite number of narrators (two, three, ten, etc.). For instance, a narrator may introduce another narrator who in turn introduces another narrator, and so forth:

> (31) I was having a cup of coffee in a dingy luncheonette when a stranger sat at my table and told me: " A few years ago — I was twenty at the time — I had a very strange experience. I was walking down the street. . .. A few years

later, a beautiful woman came to see be and told me: 'I
was. . . .'";

or a narrator may introduce another narrator, then another one,
then another one, and so on:

(32)   I was having a cup of coffee in a dingy luncheonette
when John sat at my table and told me a story: " A few
years ago, I was. . .." Then Peter came and told me
another story: "A few days ago, I was. . .." I kept drinking coffee. . . .

When there are two or more narrators in a narrative, it is possible
to establish a hierarchy among them. The one who ultimately introduces the entire narrative (including all the mini-narratives com-
prising parts of it) is the main narrator. The others are secondary
narrators, or tertiary ones, etc. In (31), the first 'I' is the main
narrator, the stranger is a secondary one, and the beautiful woman
a tertiary one. In (32), the first 'I' is the main narrator, whereas
John and Peter are secondary ones. Note that a tertiary narrator,
for example, may be more important or interesting than a secondary one. There are three narrators in *L'Immoraliste*: the one who
provides a title for the novel and through whom all of the narrated
events are ultimately presented, Michel's friend and Michel himself.
The latter, who is a tertiary narrator, is clearly more interesting
than his friend, who is a secondary one. Finally, note that one narrator may be at a greater or lesser distance from another one, that
this distance may be physical, or intellectual, or emotional, or
moral, and that it may vary within a given narrative.

THE NARRATEE

If there is at least one narrator in any narrative, there also is at
least one narratee and this narratee may or may not be explicitly
designated by a 'you'. In many narratives where he is not, the 'you'
may have been deleted without leaving any traces but the narrative
itself. There is nothing in

(33)   She is very sick. She drinks a glass of wine and she becomes very healthy

or

(34)   Joan is very rich. She drinks a cup of coffee and she becomes very poor

for instance, which refers to or implies a narrating activity and,
therefore, a narrative audience except for the fact that they are
narratives. In many narratives where he is, the 'you' may constitute
the only reference to a narrative audience. Given

(35)   You are very sick. You drink a glass of wine and you become very healthy

we learn nothing explicit about the narratee as such, except that
he takes part in the events recounted to him: we do not know what
he thinks of these events as he is told them; we do not perceive
what his attitude towards the narrator and his narration is; and so
on and so forth. Indeed, the 'you' does not function differently
from the 'she' and the 'Joan' in (33) and (34) respectively: each
acts simply as a character's name. But there are also many narratives where numerous signs representing the narratee and signifying
his presence **in** them are evident, whether or not a 'you' designating
him ever appears.

1.   Signs of the 'You'

Some of these signs may function indirectly. Thus, just as any
'you' designating a narratee implies a narrator, any 'I' designating a
narrator implies a narratee.[5] But some — we may call them signs
of the 'you' — function more directly and represent the narratee
(and his situation). In

(36)   "We could hardly do otherwise than pluck one of its
flowers and present it to the reader" (*The Scarlet Letter*)

and

(37)   But let the one who is listening to this tale be patient. He
will find out soon enough what fate awaited John

'the reader' and 'the one who is listening' refer to an audience.

Similarly, first-person pronouns, for example, may designate not (only) a narrator but (also) a narratee. When Marcel writes in *A la recherche du temps perdu*:

> (38) "Besides, most often we did not stay home, we went for a walk"

the 'we' excludes the narratee; on the other hand, when he writes

> (39) "In such perfect coincidences, should reality apply to what we have been dreaming for such a long time, it entirely conceals it from us"

the 'we' and the 'us' include the person he is addressing. Furthermore, parts of a narrative may take the shape of questions or pseudo-questions. Sometimes, these do not emanate from a character or from the narrator, who merely seems to be repeating them. They can be attributed to the narratee. In *Le Père Goriot*, it is the narratee who asks about M. Poiret's career:

> (40) "What he had been? Well, possibly a clerk in the Department of Justice. . . ."

Sometimes, when questions or pseudo-questions emanate from the narrator, they are not addressed to himself or to one of his characters but rather to his narratee, a narratee whose opinions and experiences are thus partly revealed. In *A la recherche du temps perdu*, Marcel asks a rhetorical question to his narratee in order to explain Swann's slightly vulgar and, consequently, surprising behavior:

> (41) "But who has not seen very unpretentious royal princesses adopt spontaneously the language of old bores. . . ?"

Other passages take the shape of negations. Now, some of these do not in any way prolong a character's statement or answer a narrator's question. Rather, they contradict the beliefs of a narratee; they correct his mistakes; they put an end to his questions. The narrator of *Les Faux-Monnayeurs* vigorously denies the theory constructed by his audience to explain Vincent's escapades:

> (42) "No, it was not to see his mistress that Vincent Molinier went out every night";

and the narrator of *Les Trois Mousquetaires* explicitly contradicts one of his narratee's inferences:

(43) "D'Artagnan awakened Planchet and ordered him to open it. From this phrase — 'D'Artagnan awakened Planchet' — the reader must not suppose it was night or that day was hardly come. No, it had just struck four"

Frequently a partial negation proves to be revealing. In *A la recherche du temps perdu*, the narrator finds the narratee's assumptions about Swann's extraordinary suffering judicious but somewhat insufficient:

(44) "This suffering which he felt was unlike anything he had thought. Not only because in his hours of greatest suspicion he had rarely imagined so much evil, but because, even when he imagined this thing, it remained vague, uncertain. . . ."

There are also passages in which an affirmation by the narrator merely underlines what his narratee believes, as in

(45) "I walk for whole nights, I dream, or I talk to myself interminably. Like tonight, yes" (*La Chute*)

or

(46) Yes, the days of the Lord are mysterious indeed;

passages in which a demonstrative term refers not to an anterior or posterior element in the text, but rather to another text, another world known to both the narrator and the narratee, as in:

(47) "He adjusted his collar and the black velvet waistcoat, which was criss-crossed by one of those large gold chains made in Genoa" (*Gambara*)

or

(48) "The escaped convict gave Eugène that glance of cold compelling fascination which very magnetic people have the power of giving" (*Le Père Goriot*);

and passages in which metalinguistic or metanarrative explanations are for the narratee's benefit and function not only as signs of the 'I' but also as signs of the 'you': if I read

(49) "Afición means passion. An aficionado is one who is passionate about the bull-fights" (*The Sun Also Rises*)

I can conclude that the narratee does not know the meaning of the Spanish terms; and if I read

(50) He was wearing a yellow jacket, which meant that he was a nobleman

I can conclude that the narratee does not understand what wearing a yellow jacket signifies.

In short, any sign in a narrative which refers to a narratee's persona, his attitude, his knowledge, or his situation constitutes a sign of the 'you'. Obviously, a narratee may be represented in a more or less detailed fashion. We know almost nothing about Dr. Spielvogel in *Portnoy's Complaint* except that he is not without perspicacity; and we know even less perhaps about the narratee in "The Killers" or "Un Coeur simple". On the other hand, in *Les Infortunes de la vertu*, Juliette's entire career is presented to us; and in *Tom Jones* the narrator provides a lot of explicit information about his narratee and describes him as precisely as he does any of his characters.[6]

2.   Narratee-Character

Just as he may or may not be explicitly designated by a 'you', the narratee may be a participant in the events recounted to him (*Heart of Darkness, Portnoy's Complaint, Les Infortunes de la vertu, Le Noeud de vipères*) or he may not (*Eugénie Grandet, Le Rouge et le noir, Voyage au bout de la nuit*). When he is, we can make a distinction between the second person as narratee and the second person as character. In

(51) You ate meat

the character-you is the one who ate and the narratee-you is the one told about the eating; similarly, in *Les Infortunes de la vertu*, the Juliette to whom Justine tells her tale of woe is different from the one who achieved prosperity through vice.

Should a narratee be a character, he may — as such — play practically no other role than that of an audience in the narrative (*Heart of Darkness*). But he may also play several other roles and even function as a narrator. In *L'Immoraliste*, one of Michel's three auditors writes his brother a very long letter in which he presents his friend's narrative as well as the circumstances which led him to listen to it, and he begs his brother to help the desperate Michel. Sometimes, the narratee-character of a given account may be, at the same time, its narrator. In this case, the latter addresses this account to no one else than himself. In *La Nausée*, for example, Roquentin intends to be the sole reader of his diary and constitutes his own narratee; and the same is true of the young protagonist of *The Diary of A.N.*

The narratee-character may represent for the narrator someone who is more or less essential, more or less irreplaceable as an audience. In *Heart of Darkness*, it is presumably not necessary for Marlow to have his mates on the 'Nellie' as narratees. He could tell his story to a totally different group; he could even, perhaps, not tell it at all. On the contrary, in *L'Immoraliste*, Michel specifically needs to address his friends. Their presence in Algeria as listeners to his tale constitutes a necessary help for him, a necessary hope: they will probably not condemn him; they will understand him, maybe; they will certainly try to help him transcend his situation. Similarly, in *Arabian Nights*, Scheherazade would die if the Caliph refused to listen to her: he is the only narratee she can have.

Finally, note that a narrator may be quite mistaken in his evaluation of the knowledge, the personality, or the ability of a narratee-character. He may, for instance, describe him as not very bright and think that he can easily lie to him and mislead him, whereas another, more trustworthy narrator portrays him as particularly intelligent and well-informed. At the end of *Portnoy's Complaint*, it becomes clear that Dr. Spielvogel is not quite the narratee that Portnoy imagined.

3.   Knowledge

The narratee may know the narrator more or less well (*Heart of Darkness, L'Immoraliste*) or not know him at all (*Le Père Goriot, La Chartreuse de Parme*); sometimes too, he may know him but not recognize him: in *Les Infortunes de la vertu*, Justine and Juliette realize that they are sisters at the very end of the novel only. The narratee may also know several of the characters portrayed in the narrative (*L'Immoraliste*) or, on the contrary, he may never have heard of any of them ("Un Coeur simple"). Moreover, he may already know some of the events narrated to him and he may even have played a role in them. Michel's friends in *L'Immoraliste* are obviously cognizant of what the protagonist recounts at the very beginning of his narrative:

> (52)   "The last time we saw each other, I remember, was in the neighborhood of Angers, in the little church in which I was married. There were very few people. . . . After we left the church, you joined us at my bride's house for a short meal . . . then she and I drove away in a carriage. . ."

Similarly in *Le Noeud de vipères*, Louis refers rather frequently to various circumstances which his first narratee, Isa, knows about:

> (53)   "You told me, the other day, that I was getting to be hard of hearing . . . you alluded to my health . . . you know my laughter, that laughter which, even at the beginning of our life together, got on your nerves. . . ."

and, of course, in many diary novels, the narratee knows in advance most of the events that, as a narrator, he writes down for himself, as well as most of the characters whose actions he relates, and he takes part in most of the incidents recounted.

4.   Change

Clearly, the narratee may be more or less touched, more or less influenced by the narration addressed to him. In *Heart of Darkness*, Marlow's companions are not transformed by the story he tells them. In *L'Immoraliste*, Michel's three friends, although they are not fundamentally different from what they were before listening to him, are quite affected by his account:

> (54)   "Michel remained silent for a long time. We did not speak either, for each of us had a strange feeling of uneasiness.

We felt, alas, that by telling us his story, Michel had made his action more legitimate. Our not having known when to condemn it in the course of his long explanation, almost made of us accomplices. We felt, as it were, involved in it."

Finally, in *Le Noeud de vipères*, as in so many works in which the narrator is (or becomes) his own narratee, the latter is gradually and profoundly transformed by what is recounted.

5. Individual Narratee and Group Narratee

The narratee may be represented as a group addressed by the narrator or as an isolated individual. Michel tells the story of his life to his three friends; Marlow recounts Kurz' adventures to several of his mates gathered on the deck of the "Nellie"; and the narrator in *Gargantua* addresses many readers at the same time. On the other hand, Jean-Baptiste Clamence, in *La Chute*, tells his story to the person he meets one evening in the Mexico City Bar in Amsterdam; Roquentin, in *La Nausée*, ostensibly writes for himself only; and the narrator in "The Golden Flower Pot" always addresses one individual reader.

  The group addressed by a teller is often a perfectly homogeneous one, whose members are indistinguishable (*Notes from the Underground*). But it may also be heterogeneous. In *Werther* the editor of the letters and documents pertaining to the unhappy young hero addresses people who are likewise unhappy ("And you, gentle soul, who are suffering from the same anguish as he"), writers ("We feel obliged to suppress this passage in the letter so as not to hurt anyone, although no author need pay much attention to the opinion of one simple girl or that of an unbalanced young man"), persons with the same literary tastes as Charlotte and persons with different tastes ("Though the names of some of our native authors are omitted, he who shares Charlotte's approbation will feel in his heart who they are, if he should read this passage. And no one else needs to know"), kind hearted and perceptive women ("any perceptive female reader will be able to identify with her and understand how much she suffered"), and so on. Sometimes, the narrator addressing several categories of narratees takes advantage of this heterogeneity to clarify his message, score points or gain approval: he pits one category against the others or praises one reaction while ridiculing another. (*Werther*)

If it is not uncommon to find a narrator addressing several narratees at the same time, it is very rare to find a narrator who tells part of his story to one narratee, then another part to another narratee, and so forth. In *Le Noeud de vipères*, Louis first addresses his account to his wife Isa. He soon changes his mind and decides to write for his illegitimate son, Robert, then for all of his children. Slowly, he comes to understand that, above all, he is writing for himself and for God. What is rarer still — indeed, I cannot think of an interesting example — is a narrative in which a narrator recounts the very same events in exactly the same way to two or more different narratees in succession; or a narrative in which different narrators tell the very same story in exactly the same way to the same narratee.

6.   Hierarchy of Narratees

There are many narratives in which there is only one narratee ("Un Coeur Simple," "The Killers," "La Légende de Saint Julien l'Hospitalier"). But there are also many narratives in which there is more than one; indeed, in a given narrative, there may be an indefinite number of them (two, three, ten, etc.). When there are two or more, the one to whom all of the events recounted are ultimately addressed is the main narratee. On the other hand, one who is told only some of the events is a secondary narratee; and so on. In *La Nausée*, for instance, Roquetin, who constitutes a very interesting narratee, is not the main one in the novel; he neither knows the Editor's note preceding his diary in Sartre's work nor the footnotes by the same editors; the main narratee in the novel is capable of reading Roquetin's journal, the Editor's note and their footnotes. Similarly, in *L'Immoraliste*, we can distinguish Michel's three friends, who listen to his account, from D.R., who learns both what Michel said and one of the friends' assessment of it, and from the narratee who reads not only what D.R. reads but also the title of the novel.

As I suggested earlier, and whether it be from a moral, intellectual, emotional, physical, or social standpoint, narratees in a given narrative may be more or less different from one another. Isa, Louis' first narratee in *Le Noeud de vipères*, is very different from Robert, his second narratee: among other things, she is more truly Christian and more capable of understanding the protagonist's confession. Narratees can also be more or less similar to the narrator(s), the characters and the real readers.[7] In *La Peste*, Dr. Rieux' narratee is neither a physician nor an inhabitant of Oran; in "The Metamorphosis", unlike Gregor Samsa, the narratee never becomes a giant insect; and I am sure that the narratee described in the very first pages of *Le Père Goriot*

(You will do the same, you, my reader, now holding this book in your white hand, and saying to yourself in the depths of your easy chair: I wonder if it will amuse me! When you have read the sorrows of Père Goriot you will lay your book aside and eat your dinner with an appetite and excuse your callousness by taxing the author with exaggeration and poetic license)

is different from some of the real readers of the novel; after all, they may not have white hands, but red or black ones; they may read the novel in bed and not in an easy-chair; they may lose their appetite after having learned of the protagonist's misfortunes.

Of course, the similarities and differences between a narratee and a narrator, a character, another narratee, or a real reader, the distance separating them vary as a given narrative unfolds. Jean-Baptiste Clamence's narratee in *La Chute* becomes less and less sympathetic towards him as the novel progresses; Juliette is much closer to Justine in the final pages of *Les Infortunes de la vertu* than in the initial ones; and, towards the end of *Tom Jones*, the narrator himself underlines the fact that his relationship with the narratee has changed: they have slowly become friends.

Of course, too, these similarities and differences determine to a large extent our interpretation of and response to the narrative. Thus, many ironic effects depend on the distance between two (groups of) different narratees (*Les Infortunes de la vertu, Werther*); on the distance between narrator and narratee on the one hand and character on the other (*Un Amour de Swann*); or, on the distance between narrator and narratee (*Tom Jones*). Similarly, should a narratee be violently opposed to the narrator's values and much more or much less reliable than him, I will be encouraged to question or to endorse these values; and should two or more narratees have different reactions to a given account, I will have to determine which reaction is the sounder one.

THE NARRATION

There is at least one narration in any narrative (per any narrator!) and this narration may or may not be explicitly designated by a set of signs. In many instances, it may have been deleted without leaving any traces but the narrative itself. There is nothing in

(55)   — Where are you going?
       — To the movies!
       — Have fun!
and
(56)   Peter is very short. He takes a magical pill and he becomes
       very tall

which refers to or implies a narrating activity or its context except for the fact that they are narratives. In many other instances, however, numerous signs representing a narration (its date, its duration, its spatial context, its adequacy or inadequacy, etc.) and signifying its presence **in** the narrative are evident:

(57)   The following narration of Mary's adventures is woefully
       incomplete but it will have to do
(58)   These events occurred in less time than it takes to narrate
       them
(59)   Yesterday, November 7, 1955, Gerry celebrated his birth-
       day
(60)   In the comfortable living-room where I am relaxing, a
       handsome stranger comes in, sits down, takes out a gun,
       and shoots himself.

1.   Posterior, Anterior and Simultaneous Narration

An examination of the chronological links between the times of occurrence of the narration and the narrated yields three major possibilities.[8] The narration may follow the narrated in time, a situation occurring in a very large number of narratives:

(61)   Many years ago, John was happily walking down the street when he saw Joan. . .

It may precede it, a situation which is relatively rare and occurs in the so-called predictive narrative:

(62)   You will kill your father then you will marry your mother
(63)   Ten years from now, John will be walking happily down the street; he will see Joan. . .[9]

It may also be simultaneous with it:

(64)   John is now walking down the street; he sees Joan. . .

Note that it is sometimes difficult − with narrative jokes or recipes, for example − to determine whether the narration is posterior to, anterior to, or simultaneous with the narrated because the grammatical tenses used connote temporal indeterminacy:

(65)   A young man comes home and says: "Ma! I'm gonna get married!" "With whom?" "With Arthur!" "With Arthur? Impossible! He's Jewish!"

Note also that in some narratives − diary novels (*Désirée, Doctor Glas, The Journal of Edwin Carp*) or epistolary novels (*La Nouvelle Héloïse, Les Liaisons Dangereuses*), for instance − there are several distinct moments of narration, of which at least some occur between distinct moments of narrated. Thus events occurring at time t_1 (say, January 7th) are related at time t_2 (January 8th), then events occurring at time t_3 (January 9th) are related at time t_4 (January 10th), and so on. In this case, we speak of intercalated narration.[10]

Finally, note that the chronological relation between a given narration and the events narrated through it may vary, with the former being sometimes anterior to, sometimes posterior to, and sometimes simultaneous with the latter. At the very end of *Eugénie Grandet*, for example, the narrator says of his heroine:

(66) "Lately, there has been some question of a new marriage for her. The people of Saumur talk of her and of the Marquis de Froidfond, whose family is beginning to lay seige to the rich widow just as the Cruchot had done in former days";

and at the beginning of *Le Père Goriot*, the narrator states:

(67) "Madame Vauquer, *née* de Conflans, is an old woman who for forty years has kept a boarding house in Paris. . . ."

It is clear that the tenses used in narrating a series of events do not necessarily correspond to the time of the narrated in relation to that of the narration; to give but one example, the present tense can be used in the middle of a series of past tenses to relate certain past events more vividly.

(68) I was on Chestnut Street. Suddenly, I see a man keel over and I hear a shout. I rush towards him. It was too late, unfortunately: he was already dead.[11]

Furthermore, the fact that the narrated precedes the narration in time or follows it does not necessarily mean that a given reader experiences it as past or future. On the contrary, it is often the case that he experiences as present (transforms into a present) what is recounted as past (or future). As A.A. Mendilow says:

Mostly, the past tense in which the events are narrated is transposed by the reader into a fictive present, while any expository matter is felt as a past in relation to that presentness.[12]

If I read

(69) John took out his gun and fired

these actions may be realized as present in my imagination: at this point of the story, now, "John takes out his gun and fires." Indeed, given a series of narrated events, I will process the foregrounded (or seemingly more important) ones as present and backgrounded ones as past.

This may explain in part why certain narratologists and philosophers have argued that the preterit in a fictional narrative is not primarily an indicator of time. According to Roman Ingarden, for instance, it can function above all as the semantic expression of the ontic difference between a fictional world and the real one; for Käte Hamburger, it can label the universe of a narrative as one which exists exclusively in the mode of imagination; and for Jean-Paul Sartre, it can constitute "a present with esthetic distance. . . an artifice of *mise en scène*." It may also explain why a critic like Ramon Fernandez made the following distinction between narratives giving the impression of a present even when they use the preterit and narratives giving the impression of a past:

The novel is the representation of events which take place in time, a representation subject to the conditions of apparition and development of these events. The *récit* is the representation of events which have taken place and the reproduction of which is regulated by the narrator in conformity with the laws of exposition and persuasion. . . Thus, the essential difference is that the event of the novel takes place whereas that of the *récit* has taken place, that the *récit* is ordered around a past and the novel in a present which is not verbal but psychological.[13]

2. Temporal Distance

Whereas it is often relatively easy to determine the chronological relation between the narration and the narrated, it is rather more difficult – in fact, it is frequently impossible – to determine with any degree of precision how long before or after the narrated the narration occurs. In much (written) narrative fiction, although we are told when (at what date) the events related occurred, we are not given too many hints (or any hint at all!) as to when the narration occurs. This is true of many novels in which the narrator intrudes very little (*L'Age de raison, Le Sursis*) and in which the narrated is – as it were – presented without the mediation of a narration; but it is also true of many novels in which the narrator is very intrusive (*Sapho, The Scarlet Pimpernel*). Obviously, there are also some narratives in which the date of the narration is explicitly given whereas the date of the narrated is not:

(70)   Today, June 10, 1943, I have decided to tell the story of John and Mary. John was very happy, then he met Mary, then he became very unhappy;

and there are some in which neither the narrated nor the narration are dated in any way:

(71)   John was very rich, then he lost a lot of money and he became very poor

In some categories of narrative – the diary novel and the epistolary novel, for example – the time of the narration is often given explicitly and so is the time of the narrated. The distance between the two is then easy to compute. It may function as a device characterizing the narrator or be thematically significant. Suppose that on October 3rd a diarist writes down events that occurred on October 2nd; and that on October 4th, he writes down events that occurred on October 3rd but also some events of October 2nd which he had not recounted the day before. This is or could be an interesting fact: why did the diarist choose not to write these events down on the 3rd?; or why did he forget to write them down?; or why is he recounting them now?; or what other events of October 2nd has he not described in his diary and when – if ever – will he describe them? The answers to such questions often help to reveal the personality of the diarist, the importance of one event recounted or another, and even the overall narrative strategy of the novel under consideration.

The temporal distance between the narration and the narrated may vary. The former may become farther and farther removed in time from the latter. I start in 1950 to relate the events of 1940; I finish in 1955. On the other hand, they may slowly converge: I start in 1950 to relate the events of 1940 to 1947; I finish in 1951. Sometimes, of course, the narration may be quite distant from the narrated in time then draw nearer to it, then move away from it again, and so on. The variations in temporal distance between narration and narrated can very much influence the tone of the narrative, its developemnt, its thrust. An eighty-year old narrator recounting his life from infancy on is, in a way, much more distant from events that occurred when he was a baby than from incidents in his adolescence or mature adulthood, and this difference may be reflected in his narration. Similarly, the perspective of a narrator recounting the same events in three or four distinct temporal occasions may change, and this change may modify his narration.

3. Duration

If it is often difficult to evaluate the temporal distance between the narration and the narrated, it is frequently even more difficult to determine the duration of the former and, a fortiori, its relationship to the duration of the events recounted. When the narration and the narrated are simultaneous, there is obviously no problem; one lasts exactly as long as the other. But when they are not, the situation can be very different. In many narratives, although the duration of the narrated is specified and it is stated that the events recounted took place over a period of twenty years, for instance, or that a given event lasted twenty minutes, the duration of the narration is not mentioned at all, as if the activity took no time or were situated out of time.

Sometimes, of course, there are slight indications given about the duration of the narration and its relation to that of the narrated:

(72)   In less time than it takes us to say it, John got to the top of the stairs

But such indications are far from precise and, even if they were, they would not allow us to calculate the duration of an entire narration. In the case of intercalated narration and, more particularly, in the diary novel, there often are many references not only to the date of the narration but also to its duration. These may even be quite specific.

(73)   I have been writing for an hour
(74)   Yesterday I wrote for two hours; today I can barely hold the pen
(75)   I started this paragraph two minutes ago.

But, once again, such notations are not sufficient to express the duration of the narration taken as a whole. Even when it is not computable exactly, however, this duration may play a most important role in a given narrative. *Tristam Shandy*, for example, is based to a large extent on the fact that the duration of the narration far exceeds that of the narrated: it takes much more time to narrate events than to live them. Similarly, in Butor's *L'Emploi du temps*, Jacques Revel progressively discovers that there are simply

too many past and present events which he would like to recount
and his narration becomes more and more unable to take care of
all of them properly. Finally, in *Arabian Nights*, it is made very
clear that narration takes time; this fact is quite fortunate for
Scheherazade who manages to survive thanks to it.

4.   Space

It is practically impossible to narrate a series of events without
establishing a set of temporal or temporally bound relationships
between narration and narrated. As soon as I say

(76)   John was happy then he was sad

for instance, I indicate that the narrated precedes the narration in
time; and as soon as I say

(77)   John went to the movies then he went to the theater

I indicate that my narration reproduces the chronological sequence
of the events recounted. On the other hand, it is quite possible to
narrate without specifying any relationship between the space of
the narration and the space of the narrated. If I write a story, not
only do I not have to indicate where the events recounted take
place, but I do not have to mention where their narration occurs:

(78)   John was unhappy, then he fell in love, then, as a result,
he became happy;[14]

and even if I indicate where the events occur, as so often happens
in verbal narratives, my indications need not reveal anything about
the place of narration and need not be related to it in any significant way:

(79)   John traveled all over the United States; one day, he met
Bill in San Francisco; then, they both went to Arizona.

Indeed, the place of narration plays no role whatsoever in many
famous narratives and is frequently not even mentioned. Think of
"Un Coeur Simple." *Germinal* or *La Terre*.

However, there are written narratives — diary novels, for example
— in which the place of narration is mentioned frequently, although
it may not be significant:

(80) "I am sitting by the table. I am not going to write in this diary again until my graduation from school." (*The Diary of A.N.*)

(81) "Things are bad. I write these lines in bed. The weather has changed suddenly since yesterday." (*The Diary of a Superfluous Man*)

(82) "On my bed before me, as I write these words, is the pile of gifts with which my dear friends showered me." (*The Journal of Edwin Carp*)

(83) "The shaky penmanship of this entry is not entirely due to my excitement. Its main cause is the uneveness of The Great Western Railway Company's roadbed." (*The Journal of Edwin Carp*)

In such narratives, the place of narration sometimes functions thematically, structurally, or as a characterization device. Should a narrator only narrate when he is in wide-open spaces and near a lake, for instance, this may reveal certain features of his personality; and should another narrator tell his tale from a hospital bed, this may mean that he is very near death and that he has to rush in order to complete his narration. Furthermore, one may easily conceive of narratives in which the space of the narration is systematically contrasted with that of the narrated (I always narrate in wide-open spaces events which took place in closed spaces); or narratives in which the former is progressively more (or less) distant and different from the latter and in which, consequently, the narration is more (or less) precise (I start narrating in California events having occurred in New York; I continue my narration in Chicago; and I finish it in New York); or narratives in which the space of the narration is so peculiar that the narrated is rendered in peculiar ways (I narrate, as they happen, events which I perceive through a miniscule hole in the wall of my cell):[15]

5. Origin, Medium and Interaction with the Narrator

If the space of the narration is frequently not even mentioned in a narrative, the same is true of various other aspects of that narration, such as its origins and causes, its dialectical relationship with the narrator, and the physical medium used to deploy it. Indeed in many (written narratives, such questions as why a narrator decides to relate a series of events, what his narration means to him or comes to mean to him, and what physical shape it takes are often never raised. In many others, however, the origins of a narration are carefully explained: Scheherazade starts narrating in order to survive Jean-Baptiste Clamence does it to ease his sense of guilt; and Salavin, in *Journal de Salavin*, starts writing as part of a remarkable attempt to transform his life totally and become a saint. The interaction between a narrator and his narration may also be presented in detail: in *La Nausée*, Roquentin's writing becomes an instrument for giving time a shape, for conferring a rhythm upon a formless and seemingly interminable "present"; and in *L'Emploi du temps*, Jacques Revel's diary slowly becomes the paradoxical mirror of his victory and defeat against the malefic powers of Bleston. Finally, sometimes — in diary novels, for example — even the physical appearance of a narration and the very practice of writing are commented on:

(84) "I fear the actual paper is of rather poor quality. Already I notice that some of my heavier pen strokes are beginning to blur. However, this minor flaw is more than compensated for by the exquisitely hand-tooled leather jacket which Maude had made for it." (*The Journal of Edwin Carp*)

(85) "I write in large characters, with a brush, so that my script will be easy to read." (*The Diary of a Mad Old Man*)[16]

Perhaps one of the outstanding characteristics of modern narrative fiction is that it concerns itself explicitly with such narrational dimensions (at the expense of the narrated). Once again, however, for narrative in general, mentioning them is not essential: without some reference to narrated events, there can be no narrative, but there can be narrative without any explicit reference to narration.

6. Multiple Narrations

Up to now, I have mostly proceeded as though there were only one narration per narrative and, obviously, this is often the case. Consider , for instance, (56), (62), (71), or

(86)   John was sick, then he swallowed a magical pill, then, as a result, he became very healthy

But, even excluding cases of intercalated narration, there are many narratives in which we find more than one narration. Indeed, in a given narrative, there may be an indefinite number of them (two, three, ten, etc.) presented in (non-) chronological order. Thus, a narrator may narrate the same series of events at different times to different narratees, or different series of events — different stories, say — to the same narratee, or different series of events to different narratees; furthermore, different narrators may narrate the same events to the same narratees or different ones and they may narrate different events to different narratees or the same one.

When there are several narrations in a narrative, one of them may introduce another one which in turn introduces another one, and so on; or one of them may introduce several others in succession, and so forth. In every case, the one which ultimately introduces all of the others constitutes the main narration; the others are secondary narrations, or tertiary ones, etc. Note that a variety of links may exist between the various levels of narration in a given narrative. The links may be architectural, in case the levels develop according to related rules of construction; they may be thematic; they may be causal, when, for example, one level explains what led to the situation presented on another level; and so on. Note also that the coherence of a given narrative may thus be more or less pronounced and that its processing and interpretation (what do these different narrations have in common? why do they differ?) may be more or less complex.

THE PRESENTATION OF THE NARRATED

Any narrative obviously imparts some kind of narrated information of which the narrator is the more or less original source; he may present it in his own name, as it were, or through a character or, more generally, through a text for which he is presumably not responsible:

(87)   John had a heart attack and died on the 5th of September

(88) "John had a heart attack and died on the 5th of September," said Peter

(89) *The Topeka News*: "John had a heart attack and died on the 5th of September"

1. Explicit and Implicit Information

Much of the information imparted is explicitly asserted, that is, presented in such a way that it can be naturally questioned or denied. For instance,

(90) Paul went to the movies

is explicitly asserted since we can apply to it well-defined operations of interrogation or negation and get

(91) Did Paul go to the movies?

and

(92) Paul did not go to the movies

Much information may also be communicated implicitly: rather than being asserted, it is more or less strongly suggested through contextual, rhetorical, connotative or other means. If, for some reason, I do not wish to state something explicitly, I may imply it by saying in its place something which can be viewed as the cause or consequence of what I did not state. Thus and depending on circumstances, I may say

(93) It's raining out

to imply

(94) I don't feel like going out

and I may say

(95) John is very friendly. Did he have a lot to drink?

to imply

(96) John is friendly because he's drunk

Or else, to indicate

(97) Peter is stupid

I may use understatement:

(98) Peter is not the most intelligent person in the world

Of course, implicit information can also be imparted through syntactic structure. If I tell someone

(99)   Go get me a pastrami sandwich!

I may imply, through the command form I use, that I am superior to him since I have the right to order him around.

Note that the implicit information carried by a passage in a given text may constitute new data or a mere repetition or confirmation of data which has already been established. Moreover, like the explicit information provided, it may prove to be more or less necessary to the understanding of other passages. Finally, it may be proportionally more or less abundant:

(100)   John was very rich and Peter was very poor, then John lost everything he had, then Peter made millions of dollars and became very rich

and

(101)   John was very rich and Peter was very poor, then John lost everything he had, then Peter made millions of dollars.

may be said to carry the same information but (100) provides more of it explicitly than (101).

Note also that, because the retrieval of implicit information often depends on operations involving knowledge of the world, of social customs, of rhetorical or generic conventions, etc., different receivers of the same message may disagree as to what information that message carries implicitly. Consider, for example

(102)   John and Peter boxed ineffectually for six rounds then, in the middle of the seventh round, John knocked Peter out with a left hook. After the fight, John told the reporters: "He gave me a lot of trouble!"

To many receivers, John's statement could imply

(103)   I had a lot of difficulty connecting

but to many others it could imply

(104)   I had to carry him for more than six rounds

Indeed, divergences in the interpretation of so-called literary texts (as well as ordinary discourse) are to a large extent a function of divergences in the determination of implicit information. Of course, two different assessments of what information a text carries implicitly may be more or less valid, more or less reasonable. Should someone say

    (105)   John owned six yachts

it would be more reasonable for me to conclude that John was probably very rich than to conclude that he was twenty-seven years old. Furthermore, the assessments may be more or less interesting. Given

    (106)   Peter insists on driving a huge Cadillac even though he has no money

it is perhaps more interesting to infer

    (107)   Peter is a show-off

than

    (108)   Driving a Cadillac requires a lot of money

Lastly, they may be more or less coherent in themselves and consistent with other information imparted by the text. To say, for instance, that in

    (109)   John had no money. He went into a restaurant and he ordered caviar,
    (110)   he ordered caviar

implies

    (111)   he had a lot of money

is to disregard the rest of (109).

    In some well-defined cases, there will be no divergences in the retrieval of implicit information. In other words, this information is entirely predictable. Thus

    (112)   John is evil

is logically entailed by

    (113)   All lawyers are evil and John is a lawyer

and

    (114)   John got there at three o'clock

is entailed by

    (115)   John left at two o'clock and it took him an hour to get there

Similarly, unless the narrative explicitly indicates otherwise, two narrated (sets of) events or situations will be taken to occur at different times if "their order cannot be changed without changing the inferred sequence of events in the origin of semantic interpretation."[17] On the other hand, they will be taken to occur at the same time if their order can be changed without modifying the original interpretation. The events in

(116)   John saw Mary and fell

are not simultaneous whereas the events in

(117)   Mary drank a lot but she ate very little

and

(118)   John was happy and he was rich and he was handsome

are.

Moreover, given two (sets of) events A and B which are not simultaneous, and unless the text explicitly indicates otherwise, A will be taken to precede B in time if it appears before it. In (116) John's seeing Mary temporally precedes his fall and in

(119)   Peter went to class, saw a movie and treated himself to a
        chocolate sundae

Peter's actions temporally occur in the order of their presentation. But in

(120)   Bill went to class after he had dinner

Bill's going to class is explicitly said to follow his having dinner.

Furthermore, should events be contiguous in the space of the narrative text, they will be taken to occur in the same (general) setting unless the text explicitly indicates otherwise. In

(121)   John drank his scotch and Mary drank her beer

the setting for John's drinking is the same as the setting for Mary's drinking.

Finally, given two events A and B, and unless the text explicitly indicates otherwise, a causal connection will be taken to exist between them if B temporally follows A and is perceived as possibly resulting from it. In

(122)   It was raining very hard. John got wet

and

(123)   Mary was bored. She left the party

for example, John's wetness will be seen as resulting from the rain and Mary's leaving as caused by her boredom. According to narratologists like Roland Barthes, this is even the most fundamental way in which a series of events is truly narrativized:

> the mainspring of the narrative activity is to be traced to that very confusion between consecutiveness and consequence, what-comes-**after** being read in a narrative as what-is-**caused-by**. Narrative would then be a systematic application of the logical fallacy denounced by scholasticism under the formula *post hoc, ergo propter hoc*.[18]

Obviously, two narrative passages will differ more or less significantly depending on whether the information they carry is communicated explicitly or taken to be implicit. Consider, for instance:

(124)   It had snowed all week. Mary and Elizabeth were in a foul mood

and

(125)   It had snowed all week and, as a result, Mary and Elizabeth were in a foul mood

In (124), the narrator takes no explicit responsibility for any causal connection. He may wish to emphasize that he is merely a recorder of events and not of their relationship; he may want his audience to participate more actively in the (re)constitution of the narrative: it is up to that audience to provide what causality is needed for the narrative to reach a satisfactory degree of coherence; or again, he may be leaving himself more freedom to deny at some point any logical link between the weather and the women's mood (actually, they were in a foul mood because they had a lot of work to do). Whatever the case may be, differences in the explicitness of the information communicated can be related to differences in the functioning of the narrative. In particular, the study of what in a given narrative was (or had to be) stated explicitly and what was (or could have been) communicated implicitly can help illuminate some of the priorities of that narrative.

2. Presupposed Information

Consider the following statements:

(126)   John thinks that Peter's brother is intelligent
(127)   John realizes that Peter's brother is intelligent

It is clear that (127) carries all the information contained in (126), that is

(128)   John has a positive opinion concerning Peter's brother's intelligence

But (127) also carries information not contained in (126):

(129)   Peter's brother is intelligent

It is also clear that the semantic elements (128) and (129) are not presented by (127) in exactly the same way: (129) is put forward as something which is not in question; it is merely given as a point of reference from which one speaks, a point of reference whose nature is not to be the object of a special assertion, of a discussion, of a further development.

To express in a different way the distinction which I am trying to establish, I will say that, in (127), (128) is posed whereas (129) is presupposed and I will define the presupposition of a statement as the semantic element common to that statement, its negation, and its corrsponding yes-no question.[19] According to this definition.

(130)   John came

is presupposed by

(131)   Mary knew that John came

since it is a semantic element common to (131) and to

(132)   Mary did not know that John came

and

(133)   Did Mary know that John came?

Similarly,

(134)   Someone ate the cake

is a presupposition of

(135)   John did see who ate the cake

and

(136)   Jane Smith likes scotch

is a presupposition of

(137)   He found out that Jane Smith likes scotch.

To summarize, it can be said that a statement often imparts explicit information on two different levels, that it carries meaning in two different ways.

Saying that the presupposition of a statement is put forward as something which is not supposed to be questioned does not mean, of course, that is cannot be questioned. Should A say (127) to B, it is quite conceivable that B may answer

(138)   Is he intelligent?

or

(139)   Does Peter have a brother?

Similarly, should A say (137) to B, it is quite conceivable that B may answer

(140)   But Jane Smith does not like scotch!

or

(141)   Who is Jane Smith?

It is to be noted, however, that, in these cases – which are not uncommon – B does not develop A's primary topic (How is John? How do you know? How did he find out?) but rather begins to discuss another topic (Peter's brother, Jane Smith's drinking tastes, Jane Smith's identity). This is probably one of the reasons why B's conduct, in many circumstances, may be considered out of place: B has broken a convention of discourse according to which the presupposition of a statement does not constitute a primary topic for discussion.

Note also that, just as there are differences between posed and presupposed information, there are differences between presupposed information and implicit information. First, and most obviously, the latter **is not** stated whereas the former **is**, though not directly. It is therefore easier to deny having implied something ("Do you mean that Peter is stupid? Do you mean that John is friendly because he is drunk?" "I never said that!") than to deny having presupposed something. Second, the implicit information always depends on an explicit one: it can be understood if and only if (part of) the latter is understood first, while the reverse is not true. If I do not understand the explicit meaning of (93), (95), (97), or

(142) I would not say that he is nice

surely I will not understand what possible implicit meanings they have. Furthermore, my understanding of their explicit meaning clearly does not guarantee my understanding of their implicit meaning. This is not the case with presupposition, since it is part of the explicit meaning: saying, for example, that someone understands

(143) John still makes many mistakes
is equivalent to saying that someone understands
(144) John made many mistakes in the past
and
(145) John makes many mistakes in the present.[20]

The notion of presupposition which can help characterize the way a given statement imparts information can also help characterize the way information is presented in a given narrative. It can thus lead to a better understanding of a narrator's stance with regard to his narratee, his narration and the narrated.

When a narrator presupposes something, he – like everybody making presuppostions – puts himself in the position of someone whose audience knows (or could know) that which is presupposed. In particular, mainly through so-called presuppositions of existence – those contained in such statements as "The King of France is bald" (presupposition: there is a king of France) or "The man ate neatly and quickly" (presupposition: there is a man) – the narrator indicates (parts of) the premises for his narration, premises which he presumably shares with his narratee, which will unconditionally be taken for granted by both of them, and which indicate "what there **is**". Should a narrator begin with a statement like

(146) The young man was rich
or
(147) The little dog was barking

for instance, he acts as if the man and the dog have already been identified (or need not be) and as if the youth of the first and the small size of the second are already known. The narratee is immediately made into an insider of the world to be presented, familiar with parts of it at least, and ready to add new information (he was rich, it was barking) to the information presupposed.

Note that, although a narrator may thus postulate some sort of initial intimacy between himself and his narratee, he often chooses not to do it: the opening sections of fairy tales, for example, frequently avoid presupposition, perhaps because these tales are in no way intended to be realistic or because they are primarily addressed to an audience incapable of understanding and appreciating the technique. Note also that the (presupposition-based) intimacy may vary throughout a narrative. Finally, note that one of the ways in which a narrator may surprise us (real readers) is by contradicting what is presupposed (the man is not young: he only seemed to be; the dog is not little: he merely looked it), by violating the very elements he introduced as inviolable.

In any narrative, the narrator adopts a certain attitude towards the events he is recounting, the characters he is describing, the emotions and thoughts he is presenting. He may, for example, emphasize the importance of certain incidents and not others; he may judge certain characters outright or in a roundabout way; he may state what he thinks explicitly or without seeming to; he may take personal responsibility for arriving at certain conclusions or deny any such responsibility. Using presupposition to introduce certain kinds of information implies that this information is not new, that it is known or could be known by all, that it is not a product of the narrator's imagination or an example of his personal opinions. When Perrault writes at the beginning of *Le Petit Chaperon rouge* that the heroine "did not know that it was dangerous to stop and listen to a wolf," he gives the moral of the story without seeming to. Similarly, in "La Légende de Saint Julien L'Hospitalier," Flaubert absolves his protagonist from the murder of his parents while disclaiming responsibility for this absolution by using presupposition: "He did not rebel against God who had inflicted this action upon him." Finally, in "Un Coeur simple," which contains little direct commentary by the narrator (he is supposed to intervene as rarely as possible and keep a dispassionate, "objective" stance vis-a-vis the world of the narrated) there are quite a few (non-existential) presuppositions made and they allow the narrator to impose a certain universe of discourse, to manipulate his audience and to present certain facts as irrefutable without pointedly interrupting the flow of events. A few examples will give a more precise idea of what I mean.

At eighteen, Félicité, the heroine, goes to the Colleville assembly with a few companions. A young man invites her to dance, then: "He bought her cider, coffee, cake, a scarf, and, **not realizing she did not understand him**, offered to take her home."[21] One obvious presupposition in this passage is that Félicité does not understand the motives behind the young man's actions. Now, this is the first example of Félicité's naïveté, of her simplicity, in the narrative. The protagonist's most fundamental characteristic is thus introduced as a datum. It is presented as something that goes without saying. Félicité **is** naïveté, she **is** simplicity and that should be taken for granted.

One day Félicité saves her mistress, Mme Aubain, and her two little children from a wild bull:

This event, for many years, was a topic of interest in Pont-l'Evêque. Félicité did not derive any pride from it, **not even realizing that she had done something heroic.**

The narrator wants his audience to appreciate the protagonist's valor yet refuses to make a straightforward declaration about it. Such a declaration may, after all, seem exaggerated. More significantly, a direct statement about Félicité's heroic stature would add too important a dimension to her character. Félicité is supposed to be a "simple heart" and only "a simple heart". Indeed, the narrator's presupposition allows him to underline, rather than undermine, his protagonist's simplicity: if she does not derive any pride from her feat, it is because she is so simple that she does not even realize it is a feat.

Among the people who often visit Mme Aubain is M. Bourais, a gentleman Félicité admires:

His white necktie and his baldness, the frill of his shirt, his ample brown frock-coat, his way of taking snuff while curving his arm, **his entire person produced in her that turmoil in which the spectacle of extraordinary men throws us.**

Up to that point, the narrator has kept himself at a distance from the protagonist by never indicating that she might possibly have something in common with him. In a similar way, he has kept the narratee quite distant from her. Félicité's simplicity is an exemplary feature distinguishing her from other people. It must not, however, make her so unlike everybody else as to make her extraordinary. The narrator, therefore, has to reduce the distance between himself and Félicité as well as between her and the narratee. Through presupposition, he points out that he as well as his audience have experienced feelings very similar to those of Félicité and that this similarity barely needs to be asserted even.

The heroine attends Virginie's first communion:

When it was Virginie's turn, Félicité leaned over in order to see her; and, **with the imagination that true tenderness gives**, it seemed to her that she herself was this child; her face became hers, her dress clothed her, her heart beat in her breast.

The narrator justifies the fact that a character defined by narrow simplicity can have enough imagination to put herself completely in somebody else's place. He could do it directly, by stating that "real love endows one with great imaginative powers" and taking full responsibility for the statement. Through the presupposition, he succeeds in giving a stronger justification, without having to be held personally accountable: he is saying, in effect, that the relationship between love and imagination is so well accepted, so evident, that it can be mentioned simply in passing.

Presupposition even helps a narrator preserve a certain restricted point of view while at the same time assuring his audience of the reliability of that point of view. Virginie dies of a lung ailment and, for two nights, Félicité sits by the body:

At the end of the first vigil, **she noticed that the face had turned yellow, the lips became blue, the nose was pinched, the eyes were sunken.**

The narrator presents events according to Félicité's perspective. At the same time, the presupposition allows him to indicate that the protagonist is not hallucinating out of despair and that Virginie's body has indeed changed the way Félicité sees it has. On the one hand, the point of view is hers; on the other, it is not; anybody could have noticed what Félicité noticed.

The study of presupposition can thus help illuminate the manipulation of point of view, the control of distance, the nature of justifications and motivations. Indeed, given any narrative, the study of which information is (given as) old or shared and which is (given as) new and unshared can lead to a firmer and deeper comprehension of its functioning.

3.   Modes of Discourse

The information imparted about the world of the narrated refers to non-verbal events and situations and/or (some of) the verbal acts of a series of characters, i.e., anything the latter express in words, whether to themselves – when they are "thinking", for instance – or to someone other than themselves. There are, of course, various ways in which non-verbal events and situations can be recounted: in more or less detail, according to this or that point of view, through this or that character, and so on and so forth. There are also various ways in which verbal acts can be represented. Suppose, for example, that a given character said (to himself) at one point

(148)   I will go there at five p.m. and kill him

The narrator may neglect to report that the character expressed himself in words and simply relate the verbal event as if it were a non-verbal one:

(149)   He decided to kill him in the afternoon

(149) is an example of narrativized discourse, that is, of a discourse **about** words equivalent to a discourse **not about** words. But the narrator may also report (148) as a verbal event and he may present the character's words directly or indirectly:

(150)   I will go there at five p.m. and kill him
(151)   He said (to himself): "I will go there at five p.m. and kill him"
(152)   He would go there at five p.m. and kill him
(153)   He said (to himself) that he would go there at five p.m. and kill him

(150)–(153) are examples of free direct discourse, normal direct discourse, free indirect discourse, and normal indirect discourse respectively.[22] In (150), which is exactly equivalent to (148), the character himself "says" his own words. In (151), the situation is similar; however, the narrator explicitly points out that the character himself is to say his own words. In (152), the character himself does not say his own words; rather, as the pronouns and tense indicate, the narrator reports in the third person what the character said. In (153), the narrator does the same thing and he points that out explicitly. Note that a distinction can be made between a case of free direct discourse when the character utters a series of sentences and a case where he formulates them without uttering them. The latter constitutes what is often referred to as interior monologue. Note also that, when introduced as free direct discourse, a character's thoughts may be expressed in language which does not respect the rules of morphology and syntax. Punctuation is absent, grammatical forms are truncated, short incomplete sentences abound, and neologisms are frequent.[23] In this case – the most famous example of which is Molly Bloom's monologue – we speak of stream of consciousness.[24]

In a given narrative, a narrator may use any of the modes of discourse mentioned above: some novels and short stories are entirely written in free direct discourse (*Les Lauriers sont coupés*), some rely heavily on free indirect discourse ("Un Coeur simple"), some favor normal direct discourse (*Brothers and Sisters*), and so on. Depending on the kind of discourse adopted, the narrator and his narratee (as well as the real reader) are placed more or less at a distance from the characters and their verbal acts, with narrativized discourse creating the greatest distance and free direct discourse resulting in the smallest one. Furthermore, it is more or less difficult to interpret and recast a character's utterance as a narrated event among others. In the case of narrativized discourse, there is obviously no particular difficulty since the narrator has done the work for me, as it were; at the other extreme, with free direct discourse, the recasting and interpretation are entirely up to me.

4. Order

Events can be recounted in the order of their occurrence or in a different order. If A temporally precedes B which in turn precedes C, I may, for example, present A first, then B, then C:

(154)   John washed, then he ate, then he slept

We then say that narrated order (or story line, or *fable*, to use Russian Formalist terminology) and narrating order (or plot, or *sujet*) are identical. But I may also present B before A and C, or C before A and B:

(155)   John ate after he washed, then he slept
(156)   John slept after he washed and ate

In this case, story line and plot are clearly distinct.[25]

On the level of the narrated, events are linked chronologically in two fundamental ways: (partial) simultaneity and succession. The narrator can easily preserve the order of succession. In verbal narrative, however, and because of the very nature of language, the narrator cannot really preserve simultaneity; he can only indicate it, for instance by means of conjunctions and adverbial expressions such as 'and', 'meanwhile', or 'at the same time': in

(157)   John went down at the same time as Mary went up and Bill went out

it is clear that the first event, although simultaneous with the other two, is presented before them.

When the narrator presents an event or a series of events before its time, as it were, we have an example of anticipation:

(158)   John became furious. Ten years later, he would come to regret it. Now, he did not think of the consequences and began to shout hysterically

When he presents an event or a series of events after its time, we have an example of retrospection:

(159)   John became furious. Ten years earlier, he had vowed never to lose his temper. Now, he forgot all of his resolutions and he began to shout hysterically

These distortions in the chronology of the narrated may, of course, be more or less important and more or less complicated. A given event or series of events may be displaced a few seconds only or a few years in time; furthermore, the displacement may involve very few events lasting a minute or an hour, but it may also involve very many events lasting a month, a year, or twenty years; and some anticipations may occur within retrospections or vice versa.

When the distortions are important, the terms 'flashback' (going back in time) and 'flashforward' (going forward in time) are often used. These have cinematic connotations — especially the first one — even though countless examples of flashback and flashforward can be found in verbal narratives antedating the birth of the movies and even though retrospections and anticipations are handled much more easily and efficiently in (written) verbal narrative. The medium does affect the presentation. Flashforwards are very rare in films and their use in relatively recent works (*Petulia, They Shoot Horses, Don't They*) has been cumbersome and ineffective. As for flashbacks, or even flashbacks within flashbacks, they do occur rather often in films (*The Locket*) but less frequently than in written narratives: too great a number of them would tend to confuse the viewer. A reader can go back a few pages; a viewer usually cannot go back a few frames. A writer can easily indicate whether or not a series of events precedes or follows another in time; a movie director cannot.

As I have suggested, the difference between *fable* and *sujet* can be more or less significant. The more pronounced it is, the more difficult it will be to process the narrated events in their "original" order. Moreover, any such difference can affect my interpretation of and response to a given narrative; after all, it may help highlight certain events as opposed to others; it may underline certain themes; it may help create suspense (what happened first is revealed only at the very end); and, in general, it may be more or less aesthetically pleasing and engage my emotions more or less powerfully.

5.   Point of View

Whenever we narrate, we adopt a certain (perceptual and psychological) point of view in our presentation of the narrated. Thus, we may describe a given character from the outside, as an impartial onlooker would; or we may describe the same character as he himself would; or we may describe him not only from the outside but also from the inside, as an omniscient being would; and so on and so forth.

There are three main types of point of view possible in narrative.[26] The first type, which is characteristic of "traditional" or "classical" narrative (*Le Chevalier à la charrette, Vanity Fair* or *Adam Bede*, for example) may be called unrestricted (unsituated) point of view because there is no restriction whatsoever placed upon what a narrator may describe in terms of it. As Norman Friedman wrote, the narrated may then

be seen from any or all angles at will: from a godlike vantage point beyond time and place, from the center, the periphery or front. There is nothing to keep the author [the narrator] from choosing any of them, or from shifting from one to the other as often or rarely as he pleases.[27]

In this case, the narrator tells more than any and all the characters (could) know and tell at the time of the situation described:

(160) He never realized that this was the beginning of his downfall

(161) In 1800, he met the man who defeated Napoleon at Waterloo

(162) She did not see him hiding in the bushes and laughing

He is often referred to as omniscient although — strictly speaking — the term is not always quite appropriate. Indeed, so-called omniscient narrators frequently indicate that they do not know everything:

(163) "I know not, be it remarked by the way, whether this is not the same cell, the interior of which may still be seen through a small square aperture on the east side, at about the height of a man, on the platforms from which the towers rise" (*Notre-Dame de Paris*)

(164) "Could he have been the receiver of beasts at a slaughterhouse; or a sub-inspector of public health and sewers? Whatever his occupation, he was surely one of the asses which are not used to turn the mill of our system of civilization" (*Le Père Goriot*)

The second type may be called internal point of view; everything is presented strictly in terms of the knowledge, feelings, and perceptions of one or several characters (*Vengeance is Mine, A Deadly*

Shade of Gold, La Mort dans l'âme, Le Sursis). In this case, the narrator tells only what one or several characters (could) know and tell. Internal point of view may be fixed (when the perspective of one and only one character is adopted, as in *What Maisie Knew*), variable (when the perspective of several characters is adopted in turn to present several different sequences of events, as in *The Golden Bowl* and *L'Age de raison*), or multiple (when the same event or series of events, is narrated more than once, each time in terms of a different perspective, as in *The Moonstone* and *The Ring and the Book*).

The third type — which is characteristic of "objective" or "behaviorist" narratives like "The Killers" and "Hills Like White Elephants" — may be called external point of view. Here the narrator presents everything strictly from the outside; thus, he would describe a given character's actions or physical appearance, for instance, but he would not describe the character's feelings or thoughts. Obviously, the narrator then tells less about certain situations than one or several characters (could) know and tell.[28]

Note that the type of point of view adopted in a given narrative may vary. Indeed, if in the case of unrestricted point of view it does not make much sense to speak of variation since, by definition, that type includes all possibilities, it is frequently in a general way only that a given narrative may be said to use internal or external point of view: strictly speaking, it is often more correct to say that, in large segments of that narrative, or in most of that narrative, a certain point of view is used. To give but one example, Sartre's *L'Age de raison* is said to adopt variable internal point of view: everything in the novel is supposed to be presented according to the perspective of one of four characters: Mathieu, Daniel, Boris, and Marcelle. Yet, at the very end of a chapter in which Daniel's point of view is used, we read:

When he emerged he was carrying in his right hand St. Michael's sword of fire and in his left hand a box of candy for Mme. Duffet.

All along, our view of Daniel and our knowledge of the situation were equivalent to his. Suddenly, we see him as he does not see himself, in an ironic light, carrying St. Michael's sword. The narrator has abandoned Daniel's perspective to adopt a godlike one and, technically, we must say of *L'Age de raison* that it **mostly** uses a variable internal point of view.[29]

Note also that the adoption of a given point of view may require of a narrator that he follow certain rules or conventions. However, the narrator sometimes violates the very rules or conventions he is supposed to respect. There are two major types of such violations. Either, as in the above example from *L'Age de raison*, too much information is given in terms of the chosen point of view; or else too little information is given: for instance, some of the actions or thoughts of a character whose point of view is adopted are not presented even though they should be. In *The Murder of Roger Ackroyd*, the narrator-character tells the story according to his own point of view without indicating in the least that he himself is the murderer. Sometimes, a narrator manages to violate a law without violating it, as it were, through the granting of special privileges to the character or characters whose perspective is followed. Suppose, for example, that I tell a story in terms of a given character's standpoint and that I endow him with supernatural powers enabling him to be in several places at the same time, to know the most intimate thoughts of the characters with whom he interacts, and to understand their most secret motivations much better than they do themselves. Although a fixed internal point of view is technically preserved, it is no longer very different from an unrestricted point of view. Throughout Giraudoux' *Bella*, the perspective adopted is that of Philippe Dubardeau; but Philippe Dubardeau is very much like an omniscient being. Similarly, if I adopt a certain character's perspective, I may place him in situations which are rather extraordinary in context so as to allow him to obtain information he could not otherwise have access to. In *A la recherche du temps perdu*, the point of view is mostly that of (a changing) Marcel; and Marcel learns certain things and has certain insights because he is very lucky, to say the least: he discovers Mlle Vinteuil's sadism, for instance, merely because he has decided to rest and because his resting-place is not very far from an open window. Likewise, in *Le Noeud de vipères*, Louis often overhears conversations which he is not supposed to overhear and he frequently witnesses events which he is not supposed to witness. In the case of Proust's novel, of course, the privileges granted

Marcel take on thematic significance: accidents can open paths to knowledge.

Finally, note that the type of point of view adopted may affect not only the kinds of events recounted and their recounting but also our processing and interpretation of them. Thus, should an external point of view be used, it is up to us to assess the feelings of the characters, the meaning of their actions, the very significance of the events presented; should a fixed internal point of view be used, it is up to us to determine whether or not it distorts the narrated and how it does it; and should a multiple internal point of view be used, it is up to us to find out which account of the narrated is the closest to the truth.

6.   Speed

Within any given narrative, the events and situations making up the world of the narrated may be presented more or less quickly and the rate at which they unfold constitutes what is called narrative speed. Note that the latter has nothing to do with the time taken to write the narrative: one writer may work very slowly and another very quickly yet both may represent the same events in the same exact words. Similarly, it has nothing to do with the time taken by the narrator in the narrative to complete his account: consider a two-page description of a battle ending with

> (165)   I started my description at nine o'clock and it is now twelve

and a two hundred page description of the same battle ending with

> (166)   I started my description at nine o'clock and it is now nine-thirty

Finally, it has nothing to do with the time taken to read the narrative. Of course, it is frequently said that certain novels "read quickly" while certain others do not and reading time can often be under the partial control of the author: he has numerous means at his disposal to make us read more or less rapidly. But saying that a novel reads quickly, that it moves fast, is usually not related to the actual time it takes to read it. Besides, some readers read more quickly than others, the same reader may read more or less rapidly in different circumstances, and there are no rules — and no authorial control — dictating what a normal reading rate should be.[30]

The speed of a narrative is equal to the relationship between the duration of the narrated — the (approximate) time the events recounted go on or are thought to go on — and the length of the narrative (in words, lines, or pages, for instance). Thus, a three-page narrative recounting three days of narrated is faster than a three-page narrative recounting two days; in the same way,

    (167)   The battle lasted an hour

is faster than

    (168)   The battle lasted five minutes;

and

    (169)   He drank a cup of coffee

is faster than

    (170)   He brought a cup of coffee to his lips, opened his mouth, and swallowed all the liquid that was in the cup

Narrative speed may be constant. Consider the following, for example:

    (171)   John sang for an hour, then he slept for an hour, then he ate for an hour

For all practical purposes, there are no accelerations or decelerations in (171); the relation between the duration of each event and the number of words devoted to recount it is the same throughout. In general, however, the speed of a narrative varies considerably and it is this variation which helps give the narrative a certain rhythm.

Five categories of speed can be distinguished. If no part of the narrative corresponds to a particular event that took time, we may speak of ellipsis and say that the narrative reaches infinite speed. Suppose for example that I tell the story of Napoleon and do not narrate anything that happened to him between 1805 and 1809.[31] If some part of the narrative corresponds to no elapsing of narrated time, we speak of pause and we say that the narrative comes to a complete stop. Suppose, for instance, that while telling Napoleon's story, I interrupt myself to mention something that has nothing whatever to do with him or his world:

(172)   Napoleon won the battle of Austerlitz in 1805. Boy! is it
getting cold in here! Anyway, he then won at Jena, etc.

Similarly, I may describe at length a character or a setting and my
description may correspond to the passage of no narrated time. In
between the extremes of ellipsis and pause, we speak of scene
when there is (some sort of) an equivalence between a narrative
segment and the narrated it represents: instead of saying nothing
about certain events or saying something in no way related to
them, for example, I reproduce them as exactly as possible. Thus,
if Mary said something to Jane, I record her saying it word for
word. Finally, we may speak of summary to cover the many cases
situated between ellipsis and scene and we may speak of stretch to
cover the many cases situated between scene and pause. Specifically,
a relatively short segment of narrative may correspond to a relatively long narrated time (or to a narrated action that is usually
completed slowly) and a relatively long segment of narrative may
correspond to a relatively short narrated time (or to a narrated
action that is usually completed quickly). For instance, Mary may
have accomplished several wondrous feats in the course of a long
journey and, instead of describing them one by one, I may simply
state

(173)   Mary traveled and did many marvelous things
On the other hand, Mary may have simply scratched her nose and,
instead of reporting the scratching as such, I may indicate all of
the elements that went into it:

(174)   She brought her fingers to her nose, etc. etc. etc.[32]

Note that an ellipsis, a summary, a stretch, a scene, a pause may
be underlined by the narrator. Consider, for instance:

(175)   I will not recount what happened during that fateful
week

(176)   It would take too much time to recount John's adventures
in detail; suffice it to say that he had many extraordinary
ones

(177)   Although it lasted no more than a few seconds it is worth
devoting the next chapter to the description of Mary's
scratching

(178)   It is worth reproducing their conversation in its entirety

(179)   At this point, it is good to stop and describe the physical appearance of the stranger.

But they may also simply be inferred. Suppose, for example, that a narrative text says nothing about any elision yet I can tell from a lacuna in the chronology or a break in the sequence of events recounted that some of the latter have gone unmentioned; I speak of ellipsis.[33] Similarly, suppose I read

(180)   John fought an exciting fight

I may speak of summary: I know that a blow by blow account of the fight could have been given (and I feel it could have been interesting). Or again, suppose I read a thousand pages describing John's drinking a cup of coffee; I may speak of stretch because I know that the same activity could be described in a few words (and I feel that it should). In other words, when we speak of ellipsis, or summary, or stretch in narrative, we may actually be referring not so much to an exact relationship between narrative length and narrated time but rather to the relationship between the former and what we know or feel it could or should be: we know or feel that things worth mentioning must have happened during an exciting fight and we know or feel that the drinking of a cup of coffee can and should be presented in much less detail. Naturally, the narrative text itself may often create or reinforce this knowledge or feeling in a number of ways: think of the many novels which stress their ties with the "real world" or consider a story in which ten exciting fights are described in detail and one is not.

Ellipses and pauses occur not infrequently in narrative. There are several famous instances of ellipsis in *Tom Jones* or *La Chartreuse de Parme*, for example, and one of the distinctive features of the modern novel is perhaps the great abundance of pauses: long stretches of a work correspond to no narrated and such elements as story or plot become quite unimportant. For obvious reasons, however, no narrative can be entirely based on pauses or ellipses. On the other hand, a given narrative could use summary, scene, or stretch exclusively. Some writers have written stories which are (almost) purely scenic in method ("The Killers", *Les Lauriers sont coupés, Cassandra*) and it is easy to devise a tale which adopts summary (or stretch) as its only mode of presentation. Nevertheless, it is often the alternation of scene and summary which characterizes narrative and, more particularly, traditional narrative fiction. Should a novelist have to describe certain events necessary to the understanding and appreciation of his novel but not — for whatever reasons — worth dwelling upon, he uses summary. On the contrary, he uses scene when his novel requires specific detailing of the actions, feelings, and thoughts of the characters. Indeed, the development of the novel form can partially be described in terms of its greater use of scene than the various narrative forms — epic, romance, tale — preceding it.

As I said earlier, there is in the case of scene (some sort of) an equivalence between a narrative segment and the narrated it represents. Such an equivalence is usually marked by the absence of any intrusion by the narrator, the careful detailing of specific events, the use of the present or preterit rather than the imperfect, the preference for point-action verbs rather than stative ones, and so on and so forth. The nature of these features, as well as the desire to emulate the theater, help explain why many scenes in fiction take the form of a dialogue. Note, however, that even in the case of dialogues, the equivalence between narrative segment and narrated is really a matter of convention: even if everything that was said by x, y and z is presented faithfully and without any comment by the narrator, the speed at which it was said and the silences which interrupted it can only be rendered approximately, if at all, in written narrative.

Whereas the possibilities for true scenes are, at best, limited, the possibilities for summary (and for stretch) are obviously very numerous: as I have already implied, the same series of events can be summarized in ten, twenty or five thousand words. There are two fundamental kinds of summary. In the first, and perhaps the most common, only some features of a series of different events are presented. In the second, only the features common to a series of similar events are given: I recount once what has happened n times. This particular form of summary, which has been called iterative narration, is the opposite of repetitive narration, a mode in which I recount n times what has happened only once. It is also different from singulative narration (I recount once, in more or less detail, what has happened n times), from elliptical narration (I recount 0 times what has happened once or more than once), and from the many possible forms of narration in which I recount m times what has happened n times (where m is different from 0, 1 and n).[34]

The speed at which the narrated unfolds clearly has implications for our processing and evaluating that narrated and for our response to the narrative as a whole. Thus, the more detailed the account of an event seems, the more foregrounded that event is and the more importance it takes. Similarly, the more frequently an event is described, the more significant it presumably is. This allows us to focus our attention on certain events and not on others. But is also allows the writer to trick us: an event that was barely described proves to be essential; another that was described at length proves to be insignificant. Of course, and all trickery aside, should we believe that a certain event does not deserve the scenic treatment it gets or that another one deserves more detailing, we will respond unfavorably.

Given any narrative, the examination of the narrating along the lines I have sketched allows us to describe it in terms that are narratively pertinent. Regardless of their esthetic force or their socio-historical context, for instance, narratives can be characterized and compared according to the kind of narrator(s), narratee(s), and narration(s) they exhibit and the modes of presenting narrated information they favor. Thus,

(181)   John was very unhappy, then he met Mary, then, as a result, he was very happy

and

(182)   John was very happy as a result of having met Mary. Before meeting her, he had been very unhappy

are narratively different (one follows chronological order in recounting events whereas the other does not) though informationally equivalent. Likewise,

(183)   I was very rich, then I lost a lot of money and I became very poor

and

(184) He was very rich, then – poor thing! – he lost a lot of money and he became very poor

are narratively different (the former is in the first person, with a non-intrusive narrator, and the latter in the third person, with an intrusive one) though thematically equivalent. On the other hand,

(185) John was sick, then he took a magical pill and he became healthy

and

(186) Mary was healthy, then she took a magical pill and she became sick

are practically identical in terms of the narrating, though different informationally.

If the study of the narrating and its various features helps account for and define the specificity of any given narrative, it also helps account for the infinite variety of possible narratives. Although the features are finite in number (a narrator may or may not be self-conscious; a narration may be anterior, simultaneous or posterior; narrated events may or may not be presented in the order of their occurrence; internal point of view may be fixed, variable, or multiple), they can be exploited and combined in infinitely many ways. Indeed, there are relatively few constraints on their possible combinations (self-consciousness presupposes intrusiveness, for example; flashbacks and flashforwards preclude simultaneous narration) and these contrasts can be stated explicitly.

But the study of the narrating has further implications and further value. In the first place, once we have determined that a particular narrative exhibits a certain kind of narrator, adopts a certain point of view or favors a certain order of presentation, we can begin to wonder why it does. In other words, we can ask not only which narrating possibilities a given text has exploited but also why it has exploited them (and how successfully or interestingly). Moreover, as I have pointed out in passing, such features as degree of reliability, variations in distance, modes of discourse, or narrative speed affect our interpretation of and response to a narrative and illuminate its functioning. Above all, it is because I can distinguish the narrating from the narrated and because I can (re)constitute the latter with the help of the former that I can begin to talk about the world represented.

CHAPTER TWO

Narrated

A narrative recounts a certain number of situations and events occuring in a certain world. More specifically, it expresses propositions — each analyzable as a topic-comment structure — about that world. Thus, given passages such as

    (1)   John was happy

or

    (2)   Mary ate an apple

we may say that each expresses one proposition (topic: John/ Mary; comment: being happy/eating and apple); given

    (3)   Shirley was good then she drifted into a life of crime

or

    (4)   Peter was rich and handsome

we will say that each expresses two propositions (topic: Shirley/ Peter; comment: being good, drifting into a life of crime/being rich, being handsome); and given

    (5)   a boy

'or

    (6)   enormous

we will say that they do not express any proposition. In other words, a proposition is a topic-comment structure expressible by a sentence, where sentence is taken to be the transform of at least one, but less than two, discrete elementary string.[1]

Note that in

(7) **"Porthos**, as we have seen, **had a character exactly opposite to that of Athos"** (*Les Trois Mousquetaires*)

(8) **"The sun**, which Du Barthes, that classic ancestor of periphrasis, had not yet styled 'the grand duke of candles,' **shone forth brightly and cheerily"** (*Notre-Dame de Paris*)

and

(9) Since I have forgotten what he looked like, I cannot describe him in detail. It is enough to say that **he was tall and handsome**

only the parts underlined express propositions about the world of the narrated. The rest does not refer to that world but to its representation and is made up of narrating signs.

Note also that each proposition pertains to one and only one event or situation.[2] Furthermore, each provides some new information about the world represented. Given

(10) John was strong: he defeated Bill. John was strong: he defeated Harry,

for instance, the double mention of John's strength expresses a single proposition (and constitutes a sign of the narrating). Finally, the set of propositions is chronologically ordered and non-contradictory.

EVENTS

Events (or the propositions pertaining to them) can be defined as stative (when they constitute a state, that is, when they can be expressed by a sentence of the form NP's V-ing (NP) Aux be a state) or active (when they constitute an action and cannot be expressed by a sentence of the form above).[3]
Consider for example:

(11) John was handsome

(12) The sun was shining

(13) Peter ate an apple

(14)   The cat jumped on the table

The proportion of active and stative events in a narrative is an important characteristic of that narrative. Thus, all other things being equal, a story in which most events are stative will be less dynamic than one in which most events are active. Realistic novels, where long descriptions of characters and settings abound, and romantic novels, where local color is important and fifty pages or more can be devoted to the depiction of Constantinople or Notre-Dame de Paris, are more static than adventure novels where descriptions are kept to a minimum and where it is mainly the action of various characters that matters. Furthermore, the distributional pattern of stative and active events in a given narrative or set of narratives no doubt helps distinguish it from other narratives or sets of narratives. In some narratives, a balance between stative and active events is maintained throughout. In others, on the contrary, stative or active events clearly predominate in certain sections. In many novels, for instance, the initial section differs from most if not all other sections in at least one way: it mainly refers to stative events because it is devoted to exposition, to giving the reader background information concerning the characters and the environment in which they live. Sometimes, the expository section of a novel can even make up an inordinately large part of that novel, as in many of Balzac's works; the following sections then seem tremendously dynamic by comparison. Of course, some novels – for example, Sartre's *L'Age de raison* – do not have any expository section.[4]

There is no upper limit to the number of events that may be recounted in a given narrative: one tale may relate fifty events, another one five hundred, still another one ten thousand and so on. There is, however, a lower limit since a narrative is the recounting of at least two events not presupposed or entailed by each other. (1) and (2), for instance do not constitute narratives, although they could be parts of one. On the other hand, (3) does.

ORGANIZATION

Temporal Relations

The events recounted in a narrative are organized along a temporal axis. Some may be simultaneous:

(15)   At eight o'clock, John got up and Mary went to sleep
(16)   The sun was shining and the birds were singing

But at least one must precede another one at a time. It follows that

(17)   John ate and Mary ate and Bill ate

is not a narrative, whereas

(18)   John ate and Mary ate, then Bill ate

and

(19)   John ate, then Mary ate, then Bill ate

are.

Should an event A precede an event B in time, the two may be temporally adjacent, or proximate, or distant:

(20)   As soon as he arrived, he started to cry
(21)   At 8:00 p.m., John got up; at 8:30 p.m., he stepped out on the front porch
(22)   Joan was born in Italy in 1925. In 1976, she left her native country for the United States

Furthermore, the duration of two non-synchronous events may or may not be equivalent:

(23)   Joan ran for an hour, then she ate for an hour
(24)   Joan ran for two hours, then she ate for three hours

and the extent of time covered by a given narrative may, of course, range from a very few seconds to indefinitely many years.

Note that, in some narratives, it may happen that certain events cannot be dated with any degree of precision and cannot be situated temporally in relation to other events. If their number is relatively small, this characteristic does not affect the chronological coherence of the narrative and it may even be quite meaningful thematically, symbolically, or otherwise. In *A la recherche du temps perdu*, the famous episode of the *petite madeleine* cannot be dated or situated properly and it is fitting in a way that it cannot since Marcel transcends time when he brings the little piece of cake to his mouth. Sometimes, certain events are dated in such a way that a few contradictions arise in the chronology. These may result from simple mistakes or oversights on the part of an author, even a meticulous one; or they may be symptomatic of his problems in handling a certain subject. In *Jean Barois*, for instance, the protagonist's daughter comes to spend a few months with him when she is 18. According to the novel, she was born in 1895 and her stay with her father should therefore take place in 1913. During her stay, however, her father – who was born in 1866 – says at one point that he is over 50: we must then be in 1916. Two years later, a friend of the protagonist says that Barois has been fighting obscurantism and intolerance for fifteen years. Since Barois started his fight in 1895, we must be in 1910! *Jean Barois* is a novel in which history plays a particularly prominent role and perhaps Roger Martin du Gard had difficulties combining historical events and fictitious ones, historical time and fictional calendar. Chronological contradictions can also be part of an overall narrative strategy and function in specific thematic and structural ways: in *La Nausée*, the final breakup between Roquentin and Anny is said by the protagonist to have occurred eight years before his keeping a diary, but also six years and four years before it; this hesitation underlines his utter detachment from the past and his sense of loss in a shapeless present. Should contradictions be very numerous in a text, it becomes impossible to establish any kind of chronology and we are then no longer in the presence of a narrative. *La Jalousie* is a case in point. Though it may, to a certain extent, function as a narrative because it adopts many of the trappings associated with narrative art, it is not a narrative since no satisfactory chronology of its events can be established. The celebrated crushing of the centipede, for example, occurs perhaps during A. and Frank's trip, before it, and after it, *La Jalousie* is a novel, of course, but a pseudo-narrative one.

2.   Spatial Relations

Just as events may be simultaneous or not, they may occur in (or pertain to) the same space or (partly) different spaces:

(25)   In the living-room, John was reading and Peter was playing solitaire

(26)   John had a beer at Jiggsy's then he had another beer at Murray's

Moreover, different spaces may be adjoining, or very near one another, or very far apart:

(27)   John walked from Ave X to Ave Y and Peter walked from Ave Y to Ave Z

(28)   John lived on Ave X and Peter on Ave Z

(29)   Joan traveled through the United States and Vera traveled through Australia

A narrative can therefore present events occurring at the same time and in the same space, or at different times and in different spaces, and so on and so forth.

3.   Causal Relations

Two events or series of events may be related not only temporally and spatially but also causally:

(30)   John was depressed therefore he started to drink

(31)   Mary felt bad because she had overslept

Indeed, in E.M. Forster's famous definition, a "plot is a narrative of events, the emphasis falling on causality."[5]

Note that, although causal connections are not an integral part of all narratives, they are characteristic of many of them. Whereas such connections are negligible in annals and chronicles, for instance, they are very numerous and significant in so-called realistic novels (*Le Père Goriot, Eugénie Grandet*). Perhaps it is Camus' *L'Etranger* which, better than any other novel, underlines the importance causality can have in a narrative. *L'Etranger* is – *grosso modo* – divided into two parts. In the first, the protagonist goes through a series of experiences connected mainly because they follow one another in time and because he is at the center of them. Meursault attends his mother's funeral, he sees a Fernandel movie, he makes love to Marie, he goes to the beach, he kills an Arab. His life is absurd, made up mostly of disparate events, and his murder of the Arab is without reason. In the second part, his judges, in order to inculpate him, try to fit his various experiences into a tightly-knit story, the culmination of which is the murder of the Arab. They do it by multiplying causal connections.

Note also that the causal links established between events may reflect a psychological order (for example, a character's actions are the cause or consequence of his state of mind), a philosophical order (every event exemplifies, say, the theory of universal determinism), a political order, a social one, and so on and so forth.

4.   Modifications

Events can be related in ways other than temporal, spatial or causal. Given two propositions pertaining to the same topic, one comment may, for instance, be the inverse of the other:

(32)   John was very happy then he was very sad

(33)   Mary ate a lot then she ate a little

or it may be its mere negation:

(34)   Mary slept well then she did not sleep well;

or it may be a repetition of it (at a different time, in a different space, etc.):

(35)   John kissed Mary at seven then he kissed her at nine

Of course, many such modifications can obtain. In particular, we can isolate modifications of manner (thus a character may – at different points – perform an action more or less well, or quickly, or happily, and so on) and modifications of modality (a wish may be fulfilled, and intention realized, a promise respected, and so forth):

(36)   John worked very efficiently then he worked a little less efficiently

(37)   Mary wanted to meet Olga and she met Olga

(38)   Harry intended to read *Ulysses* and he did
(39)   Peter promised to go and he went.[6]

5.   Relevance

Given a narrative recounting a chrono-logical sequence, where sequence is taken to be a group of non-simultaneous topic-comment
structures the last one of which constitutes a modification of the
first, events can be distinguished in terms of their relevance to
that sequence.[7] Thus, any event which is neither the one modified
nor the modified one (nor the cause of the modification) is less
relevant than any event which is. Consider, for example

(40)   John ate a hearty meal, then he took a little nap, then he
       went to work. He was feeling very happy and he met Bill
       who invited him for a drink and he accepted because he
       liked Bill. Then he met Bob and Bob was very nasty to
       him and, as a result, he felt very unhappy

Clearly, each event makes some contribution to (40) as a whole.
However, I could reproduce the entire sequence narrated, even if
I eliminated

(41)   John ate a hearty meal, then he took a little nap, then he
       went to work

Moreover, I could account for the transformation of John's happiness into unhappiness even if I eliminated

(42)   He met Bill who invited him for a drink and he accepted
       because he liked Bill

In (40), (41) is less relevant than (42) and (42) is less relevant than

(43)   He was feeling very happy then he met Bob and Bob was
       very nasty to him and, as a result, he felt very unhappy

It is partly the fact that events have different degrees of relevance
which allows us to extract a story-line (or a plot) from a narrative
and to summarize the latter: those events which are not relevant
may be omitted from an account of the story-line; on the other
hand, the first event and the last event of a sequence (as well as
the cause of the modification) may not. Given (40), (43) would

constitute an adequate summary whereas (41) and (42) would not. Similarly, given

(44) It was nine o'clock and the birds were singing and the bells were ringing and John felt strong, then he saw Mary and he felt very weak,

(45) John felt strong then he saw Mary and he felt very weak

would constitute an adequate summary whereas

(46) It was nine o'clock and John saw Mary

would not.

Furthermore, it is partly this fact which explains why various acceptable summaries of the same narrative can be given; though we would all include (a paraphrase of) the initial situation and its final modification in our account, we may summarize the events surrounding them in various ways and we may even not include them at all. Given the parable of "The Good Samaritan." for instance, we may represent the story line as

(47) A stranger was lying half dead in the road and a Samaritan helped him

or

(48) A stranger was lying half dead in the road but nobody helped him until, finally, a Samaritan came along and helped him

or

(49) A stranger was lying half dead in the road; and a priest came along but he did not help him; then a Levite came along but he did not help him either; then, finally, a Samaritan came along and helped him.

Note that, in many narratives, it is impossible to establish a hierarchy of relevance either because they do not contain any sequence or because they are equivalent to a minimal sequence. Consider

(50) John ate a hearty meal, then he took a little nap, then he went to work

or

(51)   John was good then he became evil.

In this case no story-line extraction is possible.

6.   Aggregates of Situations and Activities

In a given narrative, various events constituting more or less heterogeneous situations and activities may, when combined, constitute larger situations and activities. Depending on the context, for example,

(52)   He went skating, then he had ice-cream, then he watched a movie

could yield

(53)   He had a lot of fun

or

(54)   He wasted a lot of time

Note that this fact too partly explains our ability to summarize narratives. Suppose that we read

(55)   John suddenly punched Jim, then Jim kicked John, then they threw bottles at each other, then they calmed down and went out to have a drink and became friends once again

and suppose that we wanted to give a summary of it. We could combine the first three events into a set entitled "Fight (between John and Jim)" and the last three into one entitled "Reconciliation (between John and Jim)" and we could summarize (55) as

(56)   There was a fight between John and Jim followed by a reconciliation between them

Of course with a narrative like

(57)   John was holding on to his briefcase. He went to a beautiful tree-covered road. Then a bird flew over the trees and a girl walked by

such summarizing would be very difficult indeed since it is not at all clear how the constituent events could be combined to yield a larger situation or activity.

7. Character

Two propositions may be related because they refer to the same topic, though they assert different things about it:

(58) John was tall and he was handsome
(59) Mary went to the movies then she went home

or because they refer to different topics although they assert the same things about them:

(60) John was red and Peter was red
(61) England went to war and so did France

What we usually call a character is a topic (or 'logical participant') common to a set of propositions predicating of it at least some characteristics generally associated with human beings: the logical participant may be endowed with certain human physical attributes, for instance, and think, will, speak, laugh, etc. The nature of the logical participant is clearly not all important, though it is usually identified as a person, but should a horse be portrayed as philosophizing and should a table be described as thinking and speaking, they would both constitute characters.[8]

Note that, because there may be indefinitely many (pragmatic) presuppositions, implications and connotations to a set of propositions, different readers' descriptions of a given character may vary: the readers will all isolate the same set, for example, but they will think of different connotations. Note also that, for a logical participant to function as a character, it must be foregrounded at least once in the narrative rather than relegated to the background and made part of a general context or setting. Given

(62) There were thousands of people at the fair, talking, laughing, shouting, and John was having a lot of fun. He walked over to one of the arcades and played the pinball machines

we would, I think, be reluctant to say that it presents thousands of characters; and given

(63)   He thought of Mary who always told him to dress nicely, he thought of Joan who talked a lot about life; he thought of Bill who knew so many jokes; and he started to cry

we would hesitate to count Mary, Joan and Bill as characters.

Depending on the type of predicates that dominate, characters will be defined mainly by their actions, or by their words, or by their feelings, and so on. We may further classify them according to generic categories of which the actions, words or feelings are illustrations: in comedy, for instance, we find some who approximate the *eiron* or self-deprecator and some who approximate the *alazon* or imposter. More fundamentally, we may classify them in terms of the functions they fulfill. Thus, following Propp and in the domain of the folktale in particular, we may distinguish heroes from false heroes, villains, helpers, donors (providers of magical agents), sought-for persons, and dispatchers (sending the hero forth on his adventures); following Greimas, and more generally, we may speak of subjects (desiring an object), objects (desired by the subject), senders (motivating the desire), receivers (recipients of the object), helpers (of the subject), and opponents (of the subject);[9] and following Bremond, we may call them agents or patients, protectors or frustrators, seducers or intimidators, informers or concealers, and so forth. Even more fundamentally, we may classify them in terms of textual prominence and simply distinguish between the main character(s) and more or less secondary ones. In general, the main character is not only referred to by the greatest number of propositions, but he is also qualitatively different from the other characters (he has distinctive ways of expressing himself; he has a name whereas everybody else is anonymous; he is the only one to be associated with certain moral attitudes). He may also be functionally different (if there is a difficult task, he is the one who performs it; if there is a lack, he is the one who liquidates it). Besides, his appearance in the narrative may correspond to strategically important points, like the beginning or the end of various sequences.

Whether they are protagonists or not, senders or receivers, heroes or villains, mainly defined by their actions or by their feelings, characters can be dynamic (when they change and grow) or static (when they do not); they can be consistent (when the predicates associated with them do not result in seeming contradictions) or inconsistent; and they can be round or flat, that is, complex or simple, multidimensional or unidimensional, capable of surprising us or incapable of it.

Note that some of the attributes of a given character (his physical appearance, his intellectual and moral qualities, etc.) may be introduced contiguously, in set-piece presentations

(He was a snubnosed, flat-browed, common-faced boy enough; and as dirty a juvenile as one would wish to see; but he had about him all the airs and manners of a man. His hat was stuck on the top of his head. . . (*Oliver Twist*)

or, on the contrary, they may be scattered one by one through the narrative: in Sartre's "Intimité", for example, we first learn that Lulu has a beautiful flat belly; a little later, the fact that she has small breasts is mentioned; still later, she is said to be slim and diaphanous; then her black hair is referred to; and so on and so forth. Note also that the presentation may be orderly (physical attributes are described before psychological ones, past actions are mentioned before present ones, etc.) or disorderly. Finally, note that, although characters constitute an important dimension of narrative, they are not essential to it. Indeed, certain narratives deal entirely with non-human(like) subjects:

(64) There was darkness and there was silence, then, one day, the sun rose and the birds began to sing and the darkness and silence disappeared

(65) The water began to boil, then, as a result, the rice began to burn

8. Setting

What is commonly called a setting is equivalent to a set of propositions referring to the same (backgrounded) spatio-temporal complex. Again, different readers' descriptions of a certain setting may vary. Again too, settings may be textually prominent or negligible, dynamic or static, consistent or inconsistent, vague or precise, presented in an orderly fashion (the front of a house is described from left to right, a wall is shown from top to botton, a castle is shown from the inside to the outside, or vice versa) or a disorderly one. Like the attributes of a character, the attributes of a setting may be introduced contiguously (we then speak of a "description") or scattered one by one through the narrative. Lastly, like characters, settings are not essential to narrative although they play a very important role in many a novel or story.[10]

9.   Theme

If events can be related in that they pertain to the same character or setting, they can also be related in that they pertain to the same theme. A theme is a general thought or idea of which a set of (sub-) propositions (or a set of themes) is taken to be an illustration. Given

(66)   John loved Mary and Peter loved Nancy
(67)   Germany waged war on France and France waged war on England

and

(68)   He liked to cut the wings off flies and she enjoyed looking at people suffer,

For instance, we may say that theme is love, war and sadism, respectively.

Of course, a theme may be more or less fundamental, more or less prominent, more or less articulated and its distribution in a given narrative may vary. Of course too, the notion of theme makes it possible for us to discuss, in the most general terms, what a narrative "is about": it "is about" that theme of which all of (or most of) the other themes in the narrative are taken to be illustrations.

10.   Functional Relations

Events or sets of events which may or may not have obvious characteristics in common — they happen at the same time or at very different times, they occur in the same place or in very different places, they are transformationally related or not, they pertain to the same themes or different ones — can also be connected in terms of their function. Thus, we may find that certain disparate situations and activities are functionally equivalent in that they constitute a difficult task to be fulfilled or its fulfillment, a lack or its liquidation, an interdiction or its violation, and so on. In

    (69)   It was forbidden by the gods to go to the movies but John went to the movies

and

    (70)   It was forbidden by the government to work hard but Peter worked hard,

    (71)   John went to the movies

and

    (72)   Peter worked hard

have the same function.

11.   Multiple Sequences

Up to now, I have mainly proceeded as though there were at most one sequence of events per narrative. Obviously, this is often the case. Consider, for example, (73) and (74) in which one and only one sequence occurs.

    (73)   Jane was happy, then she met Mary, then she was unhappy

    (74)   Joan was poor, then she found gold, then she was rich

But there are many narratives with more than one sequence; indeed, in a given narrative, there may be an indefinite number of sequences (two, three, ten, etc.) having more or less in common (in terms of characters, themes, settings, etc.) and combined in various ways. Thus, one sequence may be conjoined with another one as in:

    (75)   Jane was happy, then she met Mary, then she was unhappy, then she met Joan, then she was happy again

Moreover, one sequence may be embedded into another one:

    (76)   Jane was happy and Mary was unhappy, then Mary met Peter, then she was happy, then Jane met Joan, then she was unhappy

Finally, one sequence may be made to alternate with another one.

(77)   Jane was happy and Mary was unhappy, then Jane met Joan and Mary met Iris, then Jane was unhappy and Mary was happy

Note that the various sequences may have more or less in common and make for a more or less cohesive narrative. Note also that the combinational pattern used in a narrative may constitute an important characteristic of that narrative. For instance, it may determine at least partially the rate at which various sequences unfold. If a sequence A is embedded in a sequence B, the development of B is obviously delayed. It would be delayed even more if a sequence C was embedded in A, and so on and so forth. Note, finally, that the combinational pattern used is frequently a function of the medium adopted. Alternation is rare in oral tales but quite popular in written ones. Similarly, multiple embedding seldom occurs when the medium of representation is speech or moving pictures but occurs quite commonly when the medium is writing. After all, an audience finds it very difficult to process an oral narrative or a movie in which multiple embedding and alternation abound but does not experience much difficulty in processing a written narrative organized around the same patterns.

An examination of events and their relationships allows us to characterize and compare narratives in terms of their narrated structure. Given two narratives with different propositional content, for example, identical relations may obtain among their respective propositions:

(78)   John was poor, then he met Bill, then he became rich
(79)   Peter was unhappy, then he saw a movie, then he became happy

On the other hand, two narratives may have different narrated structures although their propositional content is identical:

(80)   Joan ate an egg and Peter drank a glass of milk, then they went to the theater
(81)   Joan ate an egg, then Peter drank a glass of milk, then they went to the theater

Once we have determined that a particular narrative is characterized by certain kinds of events or a certain way of linking them, we can begin to wonder why. In other words, we can ask not only which narrated possibilities a given text favors but also why it does (and successfully or interestingly).

If the study of the narrated and its various features helps account for and define the specificity of any given narrative, it also helps account for the infinite variety of possible narratives. Not only can any consistent set of propositions be expressed narratively but the possible relations among them can be exploited and combined in infinitely many (statable) ways.

Above all, the study of the narrated gives us an insight into how we organize narratives in order to process them as well as into why and how easily we can so process them. We are able to give a summarized account of a plot not only because we can extract the narrated from a narrative but also because we can isolate relevant events and combine them into various situations and activities. Similarly, we can process a sequence as a series of states and actions pertaining to one or more characters in one or more settings because we can distinguish certain well-defined sets of topic-comment structures. Of course, some tales, short stories, or novels may prove to be more easily organizable around characters than others, more easily thematizable, more easily summarizable. Of course too, our reading experience may vary in terms of the processing possibilities. In short, the study of the narrated helps illuminate the way(s) we understand and respond to narrative and constitutes an essential step in the elaboration of a narrative grammar.

CHAPTER THREE

Narrative Grammar

Everybody may not know how to narrate well but everybody, in every human society known to history and anthropology, knows how to narrate and this at a very early age.[1] Furthermore, everybody distinguishes narratives from non-narratives, that is, everybody has certain intuitions — or has internalized certain rules — about what constitutes a narrative and what does not. Finally, there is usually agreement as to whether a given set of elements constitutes a narrative or not, just as — among native speakers of English, for example — there is usually agreement as to whether a given set of elements constitutes an English sentence or not. Thus

    (1)   He ate then he slept

and

    (2)   A man was very unhappy, then he married an intelligent and beautiful woman, then, as a result, he became very happy

are narratives, however trivial they may be. On the other hand,

    (3)   Electrons are constituents of atoms

    (4)   Boys will be boys

and

    (5)   Some critics found Blanchot's *récits* very obscure whereas all critics found Rilla's novels very clear

however interesting, are not. Indeed, people of widely different cultural backgrounds frequently identify the same given sets of elements as narratives and reject others as non-narratives and they often recount narratives which are very similar. Russian and North American Indian folktales, for instance, were shown to have features in common.[2] Besides, should I tell someone (from my own

culture or from a different one) a story, he can often not only re-
peat it but paraphrase it, expand it and summarize it; and I can
usually do the same should he tell me one. It seems therefore that,
to a certain extent at least, everybody has the same intuitions — or
has internalized the same rules — about the nature of narratives.

A grammar of narrative is a series of statements or formulas describing these rules or capable of yielding the same results (or, to
put it in different terms, a grammar describes the rules and operations that allow one to process a particular representation as a narrative: if you process x as a narrative, it is because you make use of
the following grammar or of one that is formally equivalent to it).
In other words, it systematically accounts for some of those features
of narrative which I discussed in the preceding two chapters and
which everybody (implicitly) knows. A grammar should be explicit:
it should indicate, with a minimum of interpretation left to its user,
how a narrative can be produced by utilizing a specific set of rules
and it should assign a structural description to that narrative. It
should also be complete and account for all and only possible narratives and not merely extant ones, or good ones, or literary ones.
As for sets of elements which are recognized as narratives by some
and not by others, and there are undoubtedly many such sets, a
grammar could make clear what features these sets have in common
with sets constituting fully acceptable narratives and what features
they do not have in common with them. It could also specify their
degree of grammaticalness.[3]

Note that, with the rediscovery of the Russian formalists,
with the tremendous influence exercised by linguistics on disci-
plines such as folklore and literary criticism, with the advent of
structuralism and the subsequent development of semiotics,
many narratologists have begun to formalize some of their (and
other people's!) intuitions and discoveries about narrative, in order
to understand them better and in the hope that formalization
will lead to new discoveries.[4]

Note also that, in spite of undeniable achievements, some of the
work done in the grammar of narrative is not entirely satisfactory.
In fact, its weaknesses are obvious to the very narratologists who
have presented it.[5] Just as my main purpose here is not to write a
short history of narrative grammar from Propp through Barthes

and Lévi-Strauss to van Dijk, Todorov or Bremond, my main purpose is not to submit the highly intelligent and interesting studies of narrative grammarians to a detailed critical examination. Nevertheless, I should like to point out that the weaknesses to which I have just referred seem to me to stem from and/or be related to: (a) a lack of completeness, since the grammars proposed are sometimes bound to a limited corpus and, as a result, can describe only that corpus; (b) a lack of explicitness, since the basic structural units which the grammars deal with are sometimes not identified with precision and since no procedures are given to connect (abstract) narrative structures with the symbolic systems in which they are realized; and (c) an ambition to account for certain notions – the point of a narrative, for instance, or its esthetic force – which no narrative grammar can (or should) account for: there are no great, or beautiful, or profound, or trivial narratives for a grammar; there are only narratives. It is a grammar relatively free of these weaknesses that I will now try to present.[6]

THE STRUCTURAL COMPONENT

I have already pointed out that narratives may be expressed in a variety of ways. As a matter of fact, a narrative may be rendered through language, film, pantomime, dancing, and so on. Suppose a given narrative is expressed in written language. This language may be English:

   (6)   John was very happy, then he lost all of his money, then, as a result, he became very unhappy;
it may also be French:
   (7)   Jean était très heureux, puis il perdit tout son argent et il en devint très malheureux
or any other language. Suppose the narrative is in English. It may look like (6) or like
   (8)   John lost all of his money, then, as a result, he became very unhappy. He had been very happy before

or like still another paraphrase. Furthermore, note that nonnarratives may likewise be rendered through language or film, English or French, and so forth. Thus, to use Hjelmslevian terminology,[7] neither the substance (sounds, images, etc.) nor the form (certain specific English sentences, for example) of the expression side of a narrative defines the latter as such.

Similarly, a narrative may deal with any number of subjects and any number of themes. There are narratives about love, death, money, birds, trees, and so on. There are even narratives about narratives. Moreover, a narrative, a poem or an essay may deal with the same subject and develop the same themes: there are narratives about Napoleon but there are also poems and essays about him. The subject of a narrative and the themes it deals with — or, to use Hjelmslevian terminology again, the substance of its content side — consequently do not define it as such.

Let us assume that we have a certain number of content units, each one represented by a string of symbols. Suppose, for instance, that

content unit A = John ate an apple
content unit B = Bill ate a pear
content unit C = and
content unit D = then

A group of three units arranged according to pattern P constitutes a narrative:

(9) John ate an apple then Bill ate a pear

A group of the same units arranged according to another pattern P' constitutes a different narrative:

(10) Bill ate a pear then John ate an apple

On the other hand, a group of the same units arranged according to still another pattern P" does not constitute a narrative:

(11) Then John ate an apple Bill ate a pear

Nor does a different group of three units arranged according to any pattern. Consider, for example,

(12) John ate an apple and Bill ate a pear

or

(13) Bill ate a pear and John ate an apple

We can summarize the preceding by saying that a group of units selected at random and arranged in a random fashion does not necessarily constitute a narrative. Only groups of units having certain features and arranged according to certain patterns – only groups having certain structures – can constitute narratives. The structural component of the grammar will account for these structures or, to put it in Hjelmslevian terms, it will describe the form of the content side of narrative.

1. Kernel narratives

Let us consider the set of all kernel narratives, that is, the set of all narratives recounting n events (where $n \geq 2$) and no more than one modification of a situation or state of things.[8] According to this definition , (1), (2) and

(14) John was ugly, then he went to a spa, then, as a result, he became handsome

constitute kernel narratives. On the contrary,

(15) John was ugly, then he went to a spa, then, as a result, he became handsome, then he went to another spa, then, as a result, he became ugly

is not a kernel narrative since it recounts the modification of two states (John first goes from being ugly to being handsome, then he goes from being handsome to being ugly). Similarly, (3), (4), and

(16) John was rich

are not (kernel) narratives since they refer to one event only. Finally, (5), (12), (13) and

(17) John was tall and Peter was short and Bill was of average height

are not (kernel) narratives either since none of the events they each refer to precedes the others in time.

2. Rewrite rules and the structure of kernel narratives

Just as a grammar can be built to account for the structure of all and only English sentences, a grammar can be built to account for the structure of all and only kernel narratives. This grammar will consist of a set of symbols interrelated by an ordered set of rules, each rule being of the form $X \longrightarrow Y$ (to be read: Rewrite X as Y) and only one rule being applied at a time.[9] The rules obey the following restrictions: (a) only one symbol can be rewritten in any single rule; (b) the symbol to be rewritten and the replacing string may not be null; (c) the symbol to be rewritten and the replacing string may not be identical. Suppose, for example, that I wanted to indicate that events in a narrative may be stative or active, I could write the following rules:

   1. Event $\longrightarrow$ Stative Event
   2. Event $\longrightarrow$ Active Event

For the sake of brevity and an easier handling of rules, I shall use the following set of symbols:

N	=	kernel narrative
NSec	=	narrative section, containing n episodes and one narrative episode
CCL	=	cluster of one or more conjunctive features
Nep	=	narrative episode, containing n events and one narrative event
Ep	=	string of episodes, containing no narrative episode
Ep stat	=	string of stative episodes, containing no narrative episode
Ep act	=	string of active episodes, containing no narrative episode
ep stat	=	stative episode (group of conjoined stative events belonging to the same time sequence and containing no narrative event)
ep act	=	active episode (group of conjoined active events belonging to the same time sequence and containing no narrative event)
CF_t	=	conjunctive feature of time indicating a before-after relationship between two episodes or events
sub CCL	=	proper subset of CCL, containing no conjunctive feature of time
e stat	=	stative event
e act	=	active event

Ne stat	=	stative narrative event
In Ne stat	=	stative narrative event to be modified
In Ne stat$_{mod}$	=	modified stative narrative event
Ne act	=	active narrative event (modifying In Ne stat)
CF$_c$	=	conjunctive feature indicating that one event is the consequence of the preceding event
CF$_n$	=	any conjunctive feature which is not one of time or consequence
prop stat	=	stative proposition
prop act	=	active proposition
N prop stat	=	stative narrative proposition
N prop stat$_{mod}$	=	modified stative narrative proposition
LT$_t$	=	logical term of time
LT$_c$	=	logical term of consequence
LT$_n$	=	any logical term which is not one of time or consequence

The sign + indicates the concatenation of the various symbols in a string and may be suppressed where there is no danger of confusion.

Parentheses are used to enclose optionally chosen items. For the two rules

$$A \longrightarrow B$$
$$A \longrightarrow B + C$$
(but not $A \longrightarrow C$)

we may write

$$A \longrightarrow B \ (C)$$

Alternative replacements for a symbol, one of which may be chosen at a single application, are listed vertically within braces. Thus, for the three rules

$$A \longrightarrow B$$
$$A \longrightarrow C$$
$$A \longrightarrow D$$

we may write

$$A \longrightarrow \begin{Bmatrix} B \\ C \\ D \end{Bmatrix}$$

If we wish to apply a replacement for a given nonterminal symbol (a symbol appearing on the left of the arrow) in certain contexts only, we specify it in the appropriate rule. For instance, if A may be rewritten as B only when it is in initial position in any given string of symbols, we have the following rule:

$$A \longrightarrow B/ \# - -$$

If A may be rewritten as B only when it is in final position in any given string of symbols, we have the rule

$$A \longrightarrow B/ - - \#$$

If A may be rewritten as B only when it does not precede or immediately follow C, we have the rule:

$$A \longrightarrow B/C + \ldots + - -$$

In all cases, $- -$ shows the place where the given replacement is allowed.

The set of rules describing the structure of kernel narratives — which I shall call component C, from now on — is the following:

1. $N \longrightarrow \left\{ \begin{array}{l} \text{NSec} + \text{CCL} + \text{NSec} + \text{CCL} + \text{NSec} \\ \text{Ep stat} + \text{CCL} + \text{Ep stat} \\ \text{Ep act} + \text{CCL} + \text{Ep act} \end{array} \right\}$

2. $\text{NSec} \longrightarrow \begin{array}{l} \text{Nep (CCL + Ep)}/- - \# \\ \text{(Ep + CCL) Nep} \end{array}$

3. $\text{Ep} \longrightarrow \begin{array}{l} \text{Ep stat} \\ \text{Ep act} \end{array}$

4. $\text{Ep stat} \longrightarrow \text{ep stat (CCL + Ep stat)}$

5. $\text{Ep act} \longrightarrow \text{ep act (CCL + Ep act)}$

6. $\text{CCL} \longrightarrow \begin{array}{l} CF_t + \text{sub CCL}/ \ldots + \text{Nep} + \ldots + \text{Nep} + - - + \text{Nep} \\ CF_t \text{ (sub CCL)} \end{array}$

7. $\text{Nep} \left\{ \begin{array}{l} \text{(ep stat + sub CCL) Ne stat (sub CCL + ep stat)}/- -+ \\ \ldots + \quad \text{Nep} + \ldots + \text{Nep} \\ \text{Ne stat (sub CCL + ep stat)/Ne stat} + \ldots + \text{Nep} + \\ \ldots + - - \\ \text{(ep act + sub CCL) Ne act} \end{array} \right.$

8. $\text{ep stat} \longrightarrow \text{e stat (sub CCL + ep stat)}$

9. $\text{ep act} \longrightarrow \text{e act (sub CCL + ep act)}$

10. $\text{Ne stat} \longrightarrow \left\{ \begin{array}{l} \text{In Ne stat}/ - - + \ldots + \text{Ne stat} \\ \text{In Ne stat}_{mod} \end{array} \right\}$

11. sub CCL $\longrightarrow$ $\begin{Bmatrix} CF_c \ (CF_n)/ - - + \text{In Ne stat}_{mod} \\ (CF_c) \ CF_n \\ CF_c \end{Bmatrix}$

12. e stat $\longrightarrow$ prop stat
13. e act $\longrightarrow$ prop act
14. In Ne stat $\longrightarrow$ N prop stat
15. Ne act $\longrightarrow$ prop act
16. In Ne stat$_{mod}$ $\longrightarrow$ N prop stat$_{mod}$
17. $CF_t \longrightarrow LT_t$
18. $CF_c \longrightarrow LT_c$
19. $CF_n \longrightarrow LT_n$

In other terms, the rewrite rules making up component C specify that any kernel narrative consists of three narrative sections conjoined by a cluster of conjunctive features or of two conjoined strings of stative or active episodes; each narrative section contains a string of *n* episodes and one narrative episode; each string of episodes consists of stative or active episodes; each cluster of conjunctive features consists of at least a conjunctive feature of time; and so on and so forth.

If we apply the rules of component C, we get a derivation of the structure of any kernel narrative. For example, we could get the derivation of the structure of (1), (2), (14), or

(18) John was happy, then John met Bill, then, as a result, John was unhappy

Note that in the following derivation of the structure of (18), the number at the left of each line refers to the rule of component C used in constructing that line from each preceding line:

N

NSec + CCL + NSec + CCL + NSec	(1)
Nep + CCL + NSec + CCL + NSec	(2)
Nep + CCL + Nep + CCL + NSec	(2)
Nep + CCL + Nep + CCL + Nep	(2)
Nep + CF_t + Nep + CCL + Nep	(6)

$$\text{Nep} + \text{CF}_t + \text{Nep} + \text{CF}_t + \text{sub CCL} + \text{Nep} \qquad (6)$$

$$\text{Ne stat} + \text{CF}_t + \text{Nep} + \text{CF}_t + \text{sub CCL} + \text{Nep} \qquad (7)$$

$$\text{Ne stat} + \text{CF}_t + \text{Ne act} + \text{CF}_t + \text{sub CCL} + \text{Nep} \qquad (7)$$

$$\text{Nep stat} + \text{CF}_t + \text{Ne act} + \text{CF}_t + \text{sub CCL} + \text{Ne stat} \qquad (7)$$

$$\text{In Ne stat} + \text{CF}_t + \text{Ne act} + \text{CF}_t + \text{sub CCL} + \text{Ne stat} \qquad (10)$$

$$\text{In Ne stat} + \text{CF}_t + \text{Ne act} + \text{CF}_t + \text{sub CCL} + \text{In Ne stat}_{mod} \quad (10)$$

$$\text{In Ne stat} + \text{CF}_t + \text{Ne act} + \text{CF}_t + \text{CF}_c + \text{In Ne stat}_{mod} \qquad (11)$$

$$\text{Nprop stat} + \text{CF}_t + \text{Ne act} + \text{CF}_t + \text{CF}_c + \text{In Ne stat}_{mod} \qquad (14)$$

$$\text{Nprop stat} + \text{CF}_t + \text{prop act} + \text{CF}_t + \text{CF}_c + \text{In Ne stat}_{mod} \qquad (15)$$

$$\text{Nprop stat} + \text{CF}_t + \text{prop act} + \text{CF}_t + \text{CF}_c + \text{Nprop stat}_{mod} \qquad (16)$$

$$\text{Nprop stat} + \text{LT}_t + \text{prop act} + \text{CF}_t + \text{CF}_c + \text{Nprop stat}_{mod} \qquad (17)$$

$$\text{Nprop stat} + \text{LT}_t + \text{prop act} + \text{LT}_t + \text{CF}_c + \text{Nprop stat}_{mod} \qquad (17)$$

$$\text{Nprop stat} + \text{LT}_t + \text{prop act} + \text{LT}_t + \text{LT}_c + \text{Nprop stat}_{mod} \qquad (18)$$

The derivation shows that three events (three propositions) are recounted by (18). The first event is stative and temporally precedes the second; the second event is active, temporally precedes the third and causes it; and the third event is stative and constitutes a modification of the first.

3.   Generalized Transformations and the Structure of Non-Kernel Narratives

Many narratives are not kernel narratives since they recount more than one modification of a situation or state of things. Specifically many narratives are constituted by the conjoining of one (kernel) narrative with another one; or by the embedding of one (kernel) narrative into another one; or again, by the alternation of a section of one (kernel) narrative with a section of another one. For instance, a narrative like

(19)   John was poor, then he found gold in his field, then, as a result, he was rich. Then, as a result, Peter was sad, then

he found oil in his field, then, as a result, he was happy
can be said to be constituted by the conjoining of

    (20)   John was poor, then he found gold in his field, then, as a result, he was rich

and

    (21)   Peter was sad, then he found oil in his field, then, as a result, he was happy

Similarly, a narrative like

    (22)   John was rich and Joan was poor. Then Joan made money, then, as a result, she was rich. Then John lost money, then, as a result he was poor

could be considered to result from the embedding of

    (23)   Joan was poor then Joan made money, then, as a result, she was rich

into

    (24)   John was rich, then John lost money, then, as a result, he was poor

Finally, a narrative like

    (25)   John was happy and Joan was unhappy, then John got divorced and Joan to married, then, as a result, John was unhappy and Joan was happy

may be said to result from the alternation of one event from

    (26)   John was happy, then John got divorced, then, as a result, John was unhappy

and one event from

    (27)   Joan was unhappy, then Joan got married, then, as a result, Joan was happy

It is clear that component C cannot account for the structure of non-kernel narratives. In order to account for it, it is necessary to add a new set of rules to the rules which we already have. These will be transformational and will operate on two strings, provided these strings have a certain structure.[10] The first part of a transformational rule is a structural analysis (SA) specifying the kind of strings (in terms of their structure) to which the rule applies. A rule might apply, for example, to any two strings which can be analyzed as follows:

SA: of (a):   Nep – CCL – Nep – CCL – Nep
      of (b):   Nep – CCL – Nep – CCL – Nep

The structural analysis often contains symbols like X or Y, standing for any set of elements. Suppose only one Nep must be specified in each string for the rule to operate; the structural analysis may be given as follows:

SA: of (a):   X – Nep – Y
      of (b):   X – Nep – Y

The second part of the rule specifies the structural change (SC) by means of numbers referring to the elements in the structural analysis. Thus, given SA above, 1–3 would refer to the elements in (a), 4–6 to the elements in (b) and the structural change might be:

SC: $(1-2-3; 4-5-6) \longrightarrow 1-2-3-4-5-6$

Note that, sometimes, it is necessary to describe certain conditions that must be met in addition to those specified in the structural analysis. Suppose, for instance, that, for the transformation above to apply, it were necessary to specify that 3 and 4 are not identical, we would add a condition:

(where $3 \neq 4$)

Note also that, from now on, I shall call transformational rules operating on two strings generalized transformations and I shall call their output a transform.

The structure of narratives such as (19) could be accounted for if we applied the following generalized transformation (GT_1)

SA: of (a):   X – NSec – Y
      of (b):   X – NSec – Y
SC: $(1-2-3; 4-5-6) \longrightarrow 1-2-3-CCL-4-5-6$
      (where 3 and 4 are null)

The rule indicates that a string containing a narrative section may be conjoined with a similar string by a cluster of conjunctive features. Similarly, the structure of narratives such as (22) could be accounted for if we applied the following generalized transformation(GT_2):

SA: of (a):   X - NSec - Y
        of (b):   X - NSec - Y
SC: $(1-2-3; 4-5-6) \longrightarrow 1-2-CF_{u}-4-5-6-3$
        (where 1 and 4 or 6 may be null)

The rule indicates how a string containing a narrative section may be embedded into a similar string. Finally, the structure of narratives such as (25) could be accounted for if we applied the following generalized transformation (GT_3):

SA: of (a):   NSec - CCL - NSec - CCL - NSec
        of (b):   NSec - CCL - NSec - CCL - NSec
SC: $(1-2-3-4-5; 6-7-8-9-10) \longrightarrow 1-CF_n -6-2-3-$
        $CF_n -8-4-5- CF_n -10$
        (where 2 = 7; 4 = 9)

The rule indicates how narrative sections in one string may alternate with narrative sections in another string.

Of course, the application of other generalized tranformations of conjoining, embedding and alternation to various pairs of well-structured strings would account for other types of structures. Furthermore, and although in the examples above I have shown that the structure of some narratives can be accounted for by applying a transformational rule once, there are narratives the structure of which can be accounted for only through the repeated application of a generalized transformation or through the use of more than one such rule. Generalized transformations must therefore operate in such a way that they can apply not only to strings yielded by component C but also to strings that have already been transformed; moreover, the product of a transformation should be capable of undergoing further changes. For instance, the structure of a narrative such as

(28)   John was poor, then he met Joan, then, as a result, he was rich. Then, as a result, Peter was poor, then he met Mary, then, as a result, Peter was rich. Then, as a result, Jack was poor, then he met Ethel, then, as a result, Jack was rich

would be accounted for by: (a) applying GT_1 to two proper strings;

(b) applying GT_1 to the transform thus obtained and another proper string. In other words, (28) would be shown to result from the conjoining of

    (29)   John was poor, then he met Joan, then, as a result, he was rich

and

    (30)   Peter was poor, then he met Mary, then, as a result, Peter was rich. Then, as a result, Jack was poor, then he met Ethel, then, as a result, Jack was rich,

(30) itself resulting from the conjoining of

    (31)   Peter was poor, then he met Mary, then, as a result, Peter was rich

and

    (32)   Jack was poor, then he met Ethel, then, as a result, Jack was rich

Finally, note that, like the rules of component C, generalized transformations will be finite in number and may have to be (partially) ordered. At this point, however, and until we have a more thoroughly worked out grammar, it is not possible to determine the order in which they must apply.

The structural component of the grammar, consisting of component C plus the generalized transformations, accounts for the structure of any narrative. Besides, it helps account for such features of narratives or narrative segments as cohesiveness (all other things being equal, a segment with n conjunctive clusters will be more cohesive than a segment with $n-1$), pace (all other things being equal, a segment with n episodes will move more quickly than a segment with $n-1$) and hierarchy of event relevance (narrative events, for example, are more relevant than non-narrative ones). The structural component also allows us to compare any two narratives in terms of their structure. Thus, it would allow us to show that (29), (31) and (32) are structurally identical whereas (1), (2), (19) and (25) are structurally different. However, there are many features of narratives that the structural component does not describe. Specifically, it tells us nothing about the propositional content of narratives and does not allow us to compare them in terms of that content.

THE LOGICAL COMPONENT

What I will call the logical component of the grammar allows us to do just that. It consists of clusters of semantic features constituting instances of logical terms and propositions (or, rather, primitive arguments and predicates combining into propositions). For example, it would include such clusters as "then" (instance of LT_t), "as a result" (instance of LT_c), or "John eats" (instance of proposition).

Once we have a terminal string yielded by component C (plus transformations), we can substitute for each element of the string an appropriate instance of it: given a string like

(33)   prop act + LT_t + prop act

we could substitute the proposition "John eats" for the first element, the logical term "then" for the second, the proposition "John sleeps" for the third, and obtain

(34)   "John eats" "then" "John sleeps"
(34) represents the propositional content of a narrative like
(35)   John ate then John slept

Substitution obeys the following constraints: (1) it operates on the first (letfmost) element of the string first, then on the second element, then on the third, and so on; (2) a proposition can be a substitute for an element in a string if and only if: (a) it is not identical to and does not contradict a proposition preceding it and not separated from it by "then"; (b) it is not identical to a proposition preceding it and immediately separated from it by "then". In other words, each proposition substituted will provide new information in context and the string obtained after all the substitutions are performed will be consistent; (3) a proposition can be a substitute for the element N prop stat$_{mod}$ if and only if its initial argument is identical to that of the proposition substituted for the corresponding N prop stat and its predicate is a modification of that of the latter proposition:

(36) "John is unhappy"

or

(37) "Bill is poor"

can replace an N prop stat$_{mod}$ if and only if something like

(38) "John is happy"

or

(39) "Bill is rich"

has replaced the N prop stat of the same kernel.

The logical component of the grammar accounts for the propositional content of any narrative. Furthermore, like the structural component, it helps account for features of narratives or narrative segments such as cohesiveness (all other things being equal, the more features sets of arguments or predicates have in common, the more cohesiveness obtains) and it allows us to summarize the content of any narrative (an adequate summary would include the content of the narrative events and could include the content of such events that are the causes or consequences of narrative events and such events that lead up to or proceed from these causes and consequences). Finally, the logical component allows us to compare any two narratives in terms of their content. Thus, we would say that

(40) John felt sick, then he slept for twenty-four hours, then, as a result, he felt well

and

(41) John was fat, then he took a pill, then, as a result, he was thin

have the same structure but different propositional content whereas

(42) John was good and Bill was bad, then Bill met Mary, then he became good, then John met Joan, then he became bad

and

(43) Bill was bad and John was good, then Bill met Mary, then John met Joan, then Bill became good, then John became bad

have a different structure but the same content. However, there are many features of narratives which neither the structural nor the logical component describes. Specifically, neither tells us anything about the narrating in narratives and neither allows us to compare them in terms of that narrating.[11]

THE NARRATING COMPONENT

I have already indicated that events can be recounted in the order of their occurrence or in a different order. Consider, for instance

    (44) John was happy, then John met Mary, then, as a result, he was very unhappy

and

    (45) John met Mary, then, as a result, he was very unhappy. Before John met Mary, John had been happy

I have also indicated that the recounting of a series of events may follow, or precede, or be simultaneous with these events:

    (46) John was walking down the street and he saw Joan
    (47) John will be walking down the street and he will see Joan
    (48) John is now walking down the street and he sees Joan

Furthermore, the same event (or series of events) may be mentioned several times, as in

    (49) Mary was good: she helped the poor. Mary was good: she took care of the sick

On the other hand, a given event may not be explicitly stated. Instead of writing

    (50) John was rich, then the Stock Market went down, then John became poor

I may simply write

    (51) John was rich then the Stock Market went down

Although

    (52) John became poor

is not explicitly stated and although it is not logically entailed by any (set of) events in (51) – after all, the latter could go on with something like "But John remained rich. . ." – (52) is certainly a (very) plausible consequence of (51).[12] Note that any event in a narrative may be (said to have been) deleted if and only if (a) it is not identical to (part of) another event; (b) it is not presupposed by another event (as "John was not in the room" is presupposed by "John entered the room"); (c) it is not cotemporaneous with an event by which it is implied (as "John is European" is implied by "John is French"); (d) it is retrievable on the basis of an examination of the remainder of the narrative (and its context). Thus, in

(53) John was very handsome, then he ate meat, then he ate fish, then, as a result, he was very ugly,

(54) he ate fish

cannot be deleted since it would not be retrievable. Similarly, in

(55) John was happy, then he ate fish, then, as a result, he became rich,

(56) he became rich

cannot be deleted: there is nothing in

(57) John was happy then he ate fish

which allows us to say that John's eating fish caused him to become rich. Of course, given a (cultural) context in which it is a well-known fact that eating fish usually leads to riches, (56) may very well not be stated explicitly and be retrievable for people familiar with that (cultural) context. Indeed, in many narratives, numerous events are deleted because they can be reconstructed thanks to the context. There are even (non-trivial) narratives in which only one event is expressed:

(58) Gerald Ford was one of the leaders of the Watergate conspiracy!

can very well function as a narrative if something like the following reconstruction – providing new information – is possible:

(59) Most people thought that Gerald Ford put the law above himself, then some people found out that he was one of the leaders of the Watergate conspiracy, then, as a result,

most people thought that Gerald Ford put himself above the law.

Finally, and more generally, I have indicated that a narrative consists not only of narrated but also of narrating, and that such features as point of view, signs of the 'I' or signs of the 'you' affect its form and functioning.

1. Singulary Transformations

In order to account for the narrating, it is necessary to devise a new set of rules constituting what I will call the narrating component. The rules will be transformational and will allow us to perform certain changes in certain strings or transforms provided these have certain structure. Note that whereas generalized transformations operate on two strings, the new rules operate on a single string and are singulary transformations.

The first part of a singulary transformation is a structural analysis specifying the kind of string (in terms of its structure) to which the rule applies. A rule might apply, for example, to any string analyzed as follows:

$$e \text{ act} + CF_t + e \text{ act}$$

The second part of the rule specifies the structural change by means of numbers referring to the elements in the structural analysis. Given SA above, 1, 2 and 3 would refer to e act, CF_t and e act respectively and the structural change might be:

$$SC: \quad 1\text{--}2\text{--}3 \longrightarrow 3\text{-- before }3\text{--}1$$

Like in generalized transformations, the structural analysis may contain symbols such as X or Y, standing for any set of elements. Furthermore, it is sometimes necessary to describe certain conditions that must be met in addition to those specified in the structural analysis.

The difference between narrated and narrating orders in a story such as (45) could then be accounted for if we applied to a specific string in its structural derivation the following singulary transformation (ST_1):

SA: X - Str ep - CF_t -Str ep - Y

SC: 1-2-3-4-5 $\longrightarrow$ 1-4- BEFORE 4-2-5

(where Str ep is any string of conjoined episodes and/or narrative episodes; 1 and 5 are null)

The rule shows that a string of conjoined episodes and/or narrative episodes may appear after another string of conjoined episodes and/or narrative episodes even though the first string precedes the second in time, provided that no episodes or narrative episodes precede the first string or follow the second and that the constant BEFORE is introduced to indicate the original order of elements.

Similarly, the fact that narration is posterior in (46), anterior in (47) and simultaneous in (48) would be accounted for if we applied to a specific string in their structural derivation ST_2, ST_3 and ST_4 respectively:

ST_2: SA: X - Str ev -Y

SC: 1-2-3 $\longrightarrow$ 1-2- POST -3

(where Str ev is any string of conjoined events; 1 and 3 may be null)

ST_3: SA: X - Str ev - Y

SC: 1-2-3 $\longrightarrow$ 1-2- ANT -3

(where Str ev is any string of conjoined events; 1 and 3 may be null)

ST_4: SA: X - Str ev -Y

SC: 1-2-3 $\longrightarrow$ 1-2- SIM -3

(where Str ev is any string of conjoined events; 1 and 3 may be null)

The rules show that a narration may follow, precede, or be simultaneous with any string of conjoined events provided that the constants POST, ANT, or SIM are introduced to indicate this fact.[13]

Furthermore, the multiple mention of Mary's goodness in (49) could be accounted for with the application of ST_5:

SA: X - Str ev - Y

SC: 1-2-3 $\longrightarrow$ 1-2-3-REP 2

(where Str ev is any string of conjoined events; 1 and 3 may be null)

ST_5 shows that a series of conjoined events can be recounted more than once provided that the constant REP is introduced to indicate the repetition.

On the other hand, the deletion of something like

(60) Peter became rich

from

(61) Peter was poor, then he inherited a gigantic fortune, then, as a result, Peter became rich

would be accounted for with the application of ST_6:

SA: X - CCL -Ne stat -Y
SC: $1\text{-}2\text{-}3\text{-}4 \longrightarrow 1\text{-}2_0\text{-}3_0\text{-}4$
    (where 2 and 3 are retrievable from the string; subscript o indicates that any element it is attached to is not explicitly stated in the narrative)

Of course, the application of other sigulary transformations to various well-formed strings would account for other features of the narrating (point of view, foregrounding, intrusiveness of narrator, signs of the narratee, and so on). Besides, and although in the examples above I have only shown that certain features of the narrating in some narratives can be accounted for by the single application of a transformational rule, there are many cases in which the narrating can be accounted for only through the repeated application of a singulary transformation or through the use of more than one such rule. Singulary transformations must therefore operate in such a way that they can apply to strings that have already been transformed by the narrating component; moreover, the product of a singulary transformation should be capable of undergoing further changes. Consider for instance,

(63) John found oil in his field, then, as a result, he became very rich. Before John found oil, he was very poor

and suppose that the structural component had yielded a derivation of its structure and that its propositional content had been inserted. Its narrating would be (partly) accounted for by: (a) applying ST_1; (b) applying ST_2 to the transform thus obtained. Finally, note that, like the rules of the structural component, singulary transformations will be finite in number and may have to be (partially) ordered. At this point, however, and until we have a more thoroughly worked out grammar, it is not possible to determine the order in which they must apply.

The narrating component of the grammar allows us to compare any two narratives (or narrative segments) in terms of their narrating. Thus, it would allow us to show that (62) and

(63)   John was very poor, then he found oil in his field, then, as a result, he became very rich

have the same structure and propositional content but a different narrating; or that

(64)   He went to the theater then he went to the movies

and

(65)   He will go to the theater then he will go to the movies

have the same structure but a different content and narrating; or that

(66)   Mary ate then she went out

and

(67) Joan took a shower, then, as a result, she felt good

have the same narrating but a different structure and content.

THE EXPRESSION COMPONENT

The three components I have described so far cannot yield a given narrative; they can only yield the structure, content and narrating dimension of that narrative. To obtain the latter, an expression component is necessary. This component will be equivalent to a given language – say, written English – or, rather, to its grammar and it will allow us to rewrite in that language the information provided by the other components. In other words, if we consider a particular output of the latter as a set of instructions, the expression component carries out these instructions in written English. Should there be any difference between any two sets, two different narratives are yielded.[14]

Suppose, for example, that a derivation with the following terminal string has been yielded by the structural component:

N prop stat + LT_t + prop act + LT_t + LT_c + N prop $stat_{mod}$

Suppose also that the propositional content for this string is

(68) "John is happy" "then" "John meets Mary" "then" "as a result" " John is unhappy"

Finally, suppose that a singulary transformation ST_2 has operated on the string of events recounted. The expression component would yield

(69) John was happy, then John met Mary, then, as a result, John was unhappy

On the other hand, suppose that the propositional content had been

(70) "John feels sick" "then" "John takes a shower" "then" "as a result" "John feels healthy"

and suppose that transformations ST_1 and ST_2 had operated, the expression component would have yielded

(71) John took a shower, then, as a result, John felt healthy. Before taking a shower, John felt sick

The narrative grammar I have presented consists of four major components: (1) a finite set of rewrite rules and generalized transformations accounting for all and only narrative structures; (2) a component accounting for the propositional content of any narrative; (3) a finite set of singulary transformations accounting for narrating; and (4) a component capable of translating the instructions of the other components into (a signifying system such as) written English.

As it stands, the grammar is clearly in need of much elaboration and its ultimate construction is not for the immediate future. In particular, to be fully operative, the logical component and the expression component depend on an adequate semantic theory and an adequate grammar of English, neither of which is now available.[15] As it stands, however, the grammar is capable of assigning a structural description to any narrative, of capturing many significant features of the narrating, of characterizing — to a certain extent — the nature of the propositional content and the way it may vary, and of allowing for the (limited) comparison of any two narratives. Indeed, as it stands, the grammar constitutes not only a relatively adequate descriptive and explanatory device but also a heuristic one which allows us to ask well-defined questions concerning narrative and may help us answer them: Is the stucture of folktales significantly different from that of more "sophisticated" stories? What kind of stories — in terms of structure and narrating — does a given society favor? why are some structures which are theoretically possible according to the grammar rarely, if ever, encountered in practice? what stages does a child go through in developing his ability to narrate? does an emotionally disturbed child or adult consistently favor certain patterns that a normal child or adult would not favor? The grammar can thus deepen not only our understanding of narrative but also our understanding of man.

Of course, even if it should be thoroughly worked out, the grammar would be unable to tell us everything (or, sometimes, anything!) we may want to know about such important aspects of a narrative as its characters, its themes, or its point. Although it would indicate who the characters in a narrative might be — we need only isolate the sets of propositions having a logical participant in common and containing the feature "+ human" — and although it would yield a lot of information about the makeup of these sets, it could not provide information about the connotations they would be taken to have or the roles they would be considered to play (sender or receiver? helper or opponent? informer or concealer?) Similarly, although it would indicate that certain (sets of) semantic features are more prevalent than others, it would have no way of specifying the general thoughts or ideas they would be taken to illustrate. Finally, it would be incapable of describing the point of a narrative since that point depends on the context in which the narrative is received (what is pointless in certain circumstances may be very significant in others; what has a given point on one occasion may have a very different point on another occasion). In other words, such aspects as theme, symbol or point are not the domain of narrative grammar. Because they have to be explained at least partly in terms of a receiver, they are the domain of a theory of reading.

CHAPTER FOUR

Reading Narrative

In recent years, the study of literature in general and narrative in particular has been shifting from a concern with the author or with the text to a concern with the reader. Instead of establishing the meaning of a given text in terms of an author's intentions or a set of textual patterns, for instance, students of literature have focused more and more frequently on the ways in which readers, armed with expectations and interpretive conventions, structure a text and give it meaning. Ideal readers, virtual readers, implied readers, informed readers, competent readers, experienced readers, super-readers, archreaders, average readers, and plain old readers now abound in literary criticism and we seem to have entered an age in which the writer, the writing and the written are less important than the read, the reading and the reader.[1]

But what is a reader and what is reading? Very generally speaking, reading may be defined as an activity presupposing a text (a set of visually presented linguistic symbols from which meaning can be extracted), a reader (an agent capable of extracting meaning from that set) and an interaction between the text and the reader such that the latter is able to answer correctly at least some questions about the meaning of the former. Indeed, reading a text may be said to be grossly equivalent to processing textual data gradually by asking questions of the text and answering them on the basis of it.

Note that, according to this definition, reading a text and a reading of a text need not be equivalent: the latter may consist in (and very often does consist in) a selection, development and reordering of the answers reached during the former. Similarly, reading a text and responding to it need not amount to the same thing at all. Given a subtext like

(1)   John was Jim's brother

I may fantasize all sorts of things about John and Jim — that they both were tall, dark and handsome, that they both liked to play cards, that they both excelled at sports — and I may respond to them accordingly. However, that fantasizing (and response) is not part of my reading (1) — it does not involve any extraction of meaning — even though it may occur while I am reading (1) and even though it may give rise to some of the questions I ask about the rest of the text and to some of the answers I formulate.

Moreover, it is clear that not any set of visually presented linguistic symbols can be read: some such sets — a series of randomly picked letters scattered on a page, for example, may not constitute a text. No meaning can be extracted from them. They do not make sense or, at best, they merely trace some of the limits between sense and nonsense. Likewise, it is clear that it is not enough to recognize visually presented symbols as linguistic in order to be a reader. Identifying a series of symbols as specific graphemes (corresponding to specific sounds) is not the same as extracting meaning from them and I would not say, except as a joke, that I read German (or Rumanian, or Russian) very well but that I did not understand it. Furthermore, my reading a text implies that the meaning which I extract from it is at least partly conditioned by it. Given

(2)   John was happy
and
(3)   John was old
it would be difficult for me to read them as meaning respectively
(4)   John was unhappy
and
(5)   John was young

In other words, the answers I bring to the questions I formulate must not contradict the text. Finally, reading a text implies that the questions asked are relevant. The notion of relevance demands much more attention than I can give it here. I will simply note that a question is relevant if its possible answer is relevant, that is, if its possible answer carries old and new information pertaining to the topic(s) developed by the text. Some questions are not relevant because they have nothing to do with the extraction of meaning: to ask how many consonants there are on the first page of *The Sun Also Rises* will not prove helpful for reading that page, for understanding it; other questions, as the following mock-riddle underlines, are not relevant because they cannot be answered on the basis of the text:

(6)   The third deck of a ship is 600 feet long and 200 feet wide. How old is the captain?

and still other questions are not relevant because we already know their answer. Of course, reading a text in no way implies that all the relevant questions are asked and all the possible answers found. Indeed, it frequently implies the opposite. The set of relevant questions (and answers) is often a very large one and, as I read (in order to keep on reading!), I have to select certain questions rather than others. Of course too, learning how to read is − among other things − learning how to ask more and more relevant questions. An ingenious reader is not only one who can find new answers to old questions but also one who can think of new questions.

THE CODE OF WRITTEN NARRATIVE

Relevant questions may pertain to the denotational meaning of the symbols making up a (narrative) text, their connotational meaning, their thematic or symbolic meaning, their functional meaning, their significance in terms of other textual or non-textual worlds, and the connections that can be made among the answers arrived at. Now, it is obvious that to read and understand a narrative, to ask questions and answer them, we must know much of the code in which it is framed. We would not be able to read a novel in English, for instance, if we did not know any English. To a certain extent, the code of any written narrative is thus linguistic in nature. However, it is not monolithic. It conjoins, combines and orders a set of codes or sub-codes, of groups of norms, constraints and rules in terms of which the narrative is (more or less) decipherable and understandable. Suppose, for example, that the following sentence appeared in a tale:

(7) He shook his head from left to right several times.

In order to interpret it, in order to answer a question like

(8) What did his shaking his head thus mean?

it is not enough that I know (the code constituted by) English; I must also know the meaning of the action related by the sentence. According to some cultural codes, this action implies affirmation or approval; and according to others, it implies negation, denial or disapproval. My comprehension depends, therefore, on the cultural code which I take to be framing the tale, the code in terms of which the actions, events and situations related by a set of sentences mean something in a certain cultural context.

But there is more. Many, if not all, narratives can be considered to lead from one or several questions or mysteries (why was the young man murdered? who was the murderer? how was he caught?) to their answer or solution (the young man was murdered for money; the murderer was his best friend; he was caught thanks to an ingenious stratagem). Similarly, many narratives present situations and activities which we can group into sets having certain names because we know how such situations and activities combine to yield larger ones. Indeed, as I have already indicated, this is partly what allows us to summarize a given novel or story. Moreover, many narratives contain various elements which may function symbolically (we take them for what they are and also for something greater, more general and/or more fundamental which they represent): given the appropriate context, the account of a trip from France to Algeria may also act as that of a spiritual quest (*L'Immoraliste*), the description of a garden may evoke paradise (*Candide*) and references to snow may function as references to salvation (*La Chute*). Roland Barthes consequently theorized that, whenever we read a narrative, we organize it and interpret it according to several codes or sub-codes: a linguistic code and a cultural code, of course; but also a hermeneutic code, in terms of which certain parts of a given text function as an enigma to be solved and certain others as a solution to that enigma, or the beginning of a solution, or a false solution; a proairetic code, thanks to which we group certain narrative actions into one sequence, certain others into a different sequence, etc; a symbolic code, according to which we perceive the symbolic dimensions of various passages; and so on and so forth.[2] The code of written narrative is a combination of all these codes.

Note that, whereas we know quite a lot — though by no means everything — about the nature and functioning of the linguistic code, we know very little about other codes or sub-codes framing a narrative. Consider the following, for instance:

(9) It was nine o'clock. The young woman was standing on a dark and filthy corner of 17th street. At ten past nine, it started to snow. Yet the woman did not move. She was a spy and she had to meet her boss at twenty past nine. She had decided to kill him because she hated him but she did not know how she was going to do it and she was nervous. At twenty past nine, the boss appeared. It had stopped snowing. She took out her gun and shot him dead.

For many receivers of this narrative message, the second sentence no doubt leads to certain questions (who is this young woman? what is she doing on that dark and filthy corner?); the fourth sentence functions in a similar way (why doesn't she move even though it's snowing?); the fifth sentence represents an answer to the questions raised; the sixth sentence leads to new questions (will she be able to kill him? how will she do it?); and the last sentence answers them. But the first, third, seventh and eighth sentences in no way constitute or imply enigmas or solutions to these enigmas.[3] Why is it that certain narrative passages are thus made to function in terms of a hermeneutic code and certain others are not? We can, at best, offer only the sketch of a solution. A passage can function hermeneutically if it suggests or asserts that there is a mystery to be solved; if it formulates this mystery; if it announces a (possible) solution; and if it constitutes that solution, contributes to it or represents an obstacle to it. To put it differently, a passage can function hermeneutically if it encourages questions about the identity of someone or something (who is it? what is it?), for example through a term whose reference is unknown; questions about the state of someone or something (how is it that?), for instance by implying that a given set of circumstances is abnormal and demands an explanation; questions about the outcome of an action or situation and the way this outcome is effected (how will it end up? how will it come about?); or if it provides (partial and/ or possible) answers to these questions.

Problems pertaining to the organization of a given narrative in terms of a proairetic code, a cultural code, or a symbolic one are also difficult to solve. Why is it, for example, that certain passages are viewed according to a proairetic code and certain others are not? Once again, I will only provide a general answer and say that events can function as (parts of) proairetic units if they introduce (integral elements of) an initial situation to be modified in the world of the narrated, or if they constitute activities (which may combine into larger activities) modifying the (modified) initial solution, or if they are the causes or consequences of such activities or in any way relevant to them, or if they constitute (integral elements of) the final state of the initial solution.[4]

The very complexity of the narrative code explains in part the variety of responses to and interpretations of a given text. In any narrative communicaton, it is not the narrative code as a whole — whatever it may be — which intervenes but rather what the sender and the receiver have assimilated of the code and, more particularly, what each has selected from his personal stock to encode or decode the message. These subsets of the code have more or less in common but need not be identical.[5] Given a narrative message, the sender does not always know everything that it says to the receiver, everything that it carries for him, everything that it reveals or betrays, and vice versa. Two individuals — or the same one on two separate occasions — may therefore interpret that message differently. Though they may both view various passages as constituting riddles, the passages may not be the same; moreover, though they may both group certain events into similar sequences and give the sequences similar names, they may group other events very differently or use different names for the same sequences (as I have pointed out, we do not all summarize a story-line in exactly the same way); and though they may, at times, perceive similar thematic or symbolic dimensions, they may, at other times, differ greatly as to the themes or symbolism involved. Besides, one of them may consider a given passage in terms of a proairetic code, for instance, and the other one in terms of a hermeneutic code. A passage such as

(10)   John entered a small café, asked for the telephone, dialed
         a number, spoke rather briefly, then hung up and left

could be viewed as a sequence "Telephone Call" or could lead to such questions as

(11)   Who did John call?
(12)   Why did he call from a café?
(13)   Whom did he speak to?

and so on.[6]

MAXIMAL READING, MINIMAL READING, AND NARRATIVELY RELEVANT QUESTIONS

The relevant questions that may be asked while reading are clearly varied in kind and their number, in the case of some texts at least, may be infinite. For example, given the following passage from Perrault's *Le Petit Chaperon rouge*:

(14)   "Little Red Riding Hood left immediately to go to her
         grandmother, who lived in another village. Passing through
         a wood, she met Brother Wolf who felt very much like
         eating her; but he did not dare because of some wood-
         cutters who were in the forest. He asked her where she
         was going. The poor child, who did not know that it was
         dangerous to stop and listen to a wolf, told him: 'I am
         going to see my grandmother and bring her a girdle-cake
         with a little pot of butter that my mother is sending
         her. . .'"

I may ask such questions as

(15)   Where did Little Red Riding Hood go?
(16)   What for?
(17)   Why didn't Brother Wolf eat her?

(18) Will he get another chance?
(19) Will he succeed?
(20) What didn't the poor child know?
(21) What is a girdle-cake?
(22) Does it have any special connotations?
(23) What are the connotations of the name 'Brother Wolf'?
(24) What about 'Little Red Riding Hood'?
(25) Is Brother Wolf's desire to be understood as sexual?
(26) Will the child's grandmother protect her?
(27) What is the grandmother's name?

and so forth. Naturally, even if all of my questions have a certain relevance as I am reading, I may not find any answers to them: (27), for instance, will always remain unanswered.

In view of the above, it is not easy to determine what reading maximally would be: we can only say with certainty that, for reasons which I have already indicated in passing, it does not always consist in asking all the relevant questions and coming up with all the right answers.[7] Nor does it always make very much sense to speak of the total reading (as finished product rather than ongoing process) of a given text since the set of relevant questions and answers pertaining to the meaning of that text may be infinite. On the other hand, it is not easy to determine what reading minimally would be either: we can only say that it entails the understanding of the linguistic meaning or, to put it in other terms, it entails the capacity to paraphrase and summarize the denotational content of the text (and of its constituent parts).

Note that, in the case of narrative texts, some questions are more narratively relevant than others: they specifically pertain to features characteristic of narratives rather than non-narratives. Questions about the plot, for example, questions about the chronology of the events presented, questions about what has happened and what will happen are narratively relevant whereas questions about the connotative meaning or symbolic significance of a given event are not (at least, not necessarily). Indeed, reading a text narratively (reading it "for the story") means asking above all questions that have narrative relevance — questions generally referring back to the proairetic dimension and the story-line — and finding answers to them. If attempting to read a narrative maximally involves questions and answers about any and all of its meaningful aspects, reading it minimally involves questions and answers about what happens. Given *Le Petit Chaperon rouge*, for example, and even though I may have gathered a lot of interesting data about the similarities between the mother and the grandmother, the symbolism of the wolf and the heroine's Electra complex, I will not have read it narratively if I have not processed that the wolf eats the grandmother, gets into her bed, then eats the grand-daughter too. On the contrary, I will have read it narratively merely by focusing on the chronological sequence of events and understanding it.

TEXTUAL CONSTRAINTS

Certain (sub) texts allow only one correct answer to some of the questions asked. For instance, a text like

(28)   John was twenty-five

allows only one correct answer to

(29)   How old was John?

a text like

(30)   John had no siblings

allows only one correct answer to

(31)   How many siblings did John have?

and a text like

(32)   John was very tall

allows only one correct answer to

(33)   Was John very short?

Should anybody looking at (28), (30), and (32) answer (29), (31), and (33) with

(34)   John was seventy-eight

(35)   John had three brothers and three sisters

and

(36)   Yes, John was very short

respectively, we would most probably not conclude that he was reading (28), (30), and (32) in a highly idiosyncratic manner but, rather, that he was misreading them or not reading them at all. Thus to a certain extent, at least, and as I have already suggested, the text I read acts as a constraint on my reading.

Note that the text may allow only one correct answer to a given question without spelling the answer out. Given

(37)   Harry was five years older than Joan and Joan was twenty-five

or

(38)   All professors are crazy and Mary was a professor

it is obvious that Harry is thirty and Mary is crazy. Note also that sometimes the text not only provides answers to various questions but explicitly asks questions that a reader himself might have asked anyway. In *A la recherche du temps perdu*, for example, an exquisite pleasure invades Marcel's senses when he tastes a *petite madeleine* soaked in tea and several questions are raised in relation to this extraordinary event: "Whence could it have come to me, this all powerful joy? I was conscious that it was connected with the taste of tea and cake, but that it infinitely transcended those savours, could not, indeed, be of the same nature as theirs. Whence did it come? What did it signify? How could I seize upon and define it?"; in *Les Thibault*, the narrator finds young Jacques' power over Daniel de Fontanin remarkable and writes: "Why didn't this big thoughtful boy rebel against the urchin's influence? Didn't his education and the freedom he enjoyed give him an indisputable *droit d'aînesse* over Jacques?"; and in *Le Père Goriot*, Poiret's appearance seems to require explanation: "What kind of work could have thus shriveled him up? what kind of passion had darkened his bulbous face...?" Indeed, there is at least one modern novel, Robert Pinget's *L'Inquisitoire*, which largely consists of such explicit questions and answers to them.

If the text constrains my reading by the unequivocal answers it brings to some of my questions, it also constrains it in various other ways. Thus, it may answer my questions (or the questions it itself asks) more or less quickly. In

(39)   John was getting impatient. He had been trying to reach Jim for over an hour now,

(40)   Why was John getting impatient?

is answered immediately; but in the case of *A la recherche du temps perdu*, a reader reading the novel from the first page to the last has to wait for a very long time until his (and Marcel's!) questions about the *petite madeleine* are answered. In fact, many narratives can be viewed as spaces stretching between a question and its answer and their unfolding is partly characterized by the kinds of delays they bring to the answering of the question.[8] In a classical detective story, for instance, the most important early question often centers around the identity of the murderer and the correct answer usually comes only after several other suggested answers have proven unsatisfactory.

Furthermore, the text may force me to update more or less frequently the information I gather as I read by introducing data which make some of the answers I have reached (and some of the questions I have asked) obsolete. Consider the following:

(41)   John had many friends but then he committed a crime and lost them all

(42)   Joan very much wanted to go to the party then she changed her mind

(43)   Jim was twenty-three and he was desperately in love with Mary but she wouldn't even look at him. Three years passed, three years of endless humiliation and despair. One day, as Jim was walking down the street, he saw Mary sitting dejectedly on the curb

Questions

(44)   Did John have many friends?

(45)   Did Joan want to go to the party?

and

(46)   How old was Jim

would get different answers at different points in my reading of (41), (42) and (43) respectively. Of course, the updating of information is particularly important while reading narrative texts since their temporal dimension often entails very many changes in the situations and characters presented.

Note that, sometimes, a text provides an unequivocal answer

which it later modifies because it had been the wrong one. Suppose, for example, that the information was supplied by a narrator who lied then decided to tell the truth or by one who thought that he understood a situation then found out that he did not. I may be told that John is twenty-three, then that he actually is twenty-seven, then that he is only sixteen but looks old for his age; or that Mary loved Joan then that she really hated her but disguised her hatred very well. In such cases, I may feel that I have been misled, especially if I think that the modification indicates the narrator's bad faith rather than his ignorance. There are, of course, other reading circumstances in which I may feel cheated: instead of giving me wrong information, the narrator may omit information that is essential, or he may give me too much information and lead me on a tangent; or again, he may allow me to reach certain conclusions only to tell me later that these conclusions, though most plausible, are not correct.

On the other hand, a text may prove to be particularly helpful rather than deceptive. It may remind us of information it had given us previously if this information is necessary to the understanding of some new event or situation: think of such sentences as "The reader will recall that. . .," "It is important to remember that. . .." or "As we pointed out earlier. . .." It may explain how newly provided data, seemingly conflicting with what data we have already processed, is actually not at all inconsistent with it. When, in *A la recherche du temps perdu*, Swann, who had been portrayed as most delicate, modest and discreet, acts in a vulgar manner, the narrator quickly notes that there is no contradiction: after all, "who has not seen very unpretentious royal princesses adopt spontaneously the language of old bores?"; and, in *Journal d'un curé de campagne*, when the protagonist, who is inept in dealing with people, suddenly gets the upperhand in his confrontation with the Countess, there is no inconsistency either: the text makes it clear that God is on his side. Through the use of meta-narrative signs, the text can also summarize for us a long series of events, or give us the gist of a complex argument, or indicate the relative significance of various actions, or reveal the symbolic implications of different situations. In fact, a text can comment appropriately on any aspect of its constituent parts and partially do the reader's work for him.

METANARRATIVE SIGNS

When the subject of a discourse is language, we sometimes say that the discourse is metalinguistic. Similarly, when the subject of a discourse is narrative, we may say that the discourse is metanarrative. According to this very general definition of the term, there are many kinds of discourse which may be metanarrative: a philosophical essay on the ontology of narration, for instance, a history of the Russian novel, or the present study. Obviously, a verbal narrative itself may be metanarrative: a given tale may refer to other tales; it may comment on narrators and narratees; or it may discuss the act of narration. Just as obviously, a particular narrative may refer to itself and to those elements by which it is constituted and communicated. Consider the following, for example:

(47) "There was in all this, as may have been observed, one personage concerned, of whom, notwithstanding his precarious position, we have appeared to take but very little notice; this personage in M. Bonacieux, the respectable martyr of the political and amorous intrigues which entangled themselves so nicely together at this gallant and chivalric period. Fortunately, the reader may remember, or may not remember, fortunately, that we promised not to lose sight of him." (*Les Trois Mousquetaires*)

(48) "Perhaps I shall eliminate the preceding chapter. Among other reasons, there is, in the last few lines, something that might be construed as an error on my part." (*Epitaph of a Small Winner*)

(49) "Thus, gentle reader, I have given thee a faithful history of my travels for sixteen years and above seven months: wherein I have not been so studious of ornament as of truth. I could, perhaps, like others, have astonished thee with strange improbable tales; but I rather chose to relate

> plain matter of fact, in the simplest manner and style;
> because my principal design was to inform and not to
> amuse thee." (*Gulliver's Travels*)

These self-referential aspects of narrative have attracted quite a lot
of attention recently and some theorists have successfully argued
that many a narrative ultimately discusses itself and actually constitutes a metanarrative. [9]

There is another possible definition of the term metanarrative, a
stricter and perhaps more meaningful one. In a famous statement
on linguistics and poetics, Roman Jakobson presented a rapid survey of the constitutive factors in any act of verbal communication:

The **addresser** sends a **message** to the **addressee**. To be operative the message
requires a **context** referred to ('referent' in another somewhat ambiguous
nomenclature), seizable by the addressee, and either verbal or capable of
being verbalized; a **code** fully, or at least partially, common to the addresser
and addressee (or in other words, to the encoder and decoder or the message);
and, finally, a **contact**, a physical channel and psychological connection between the addresser and the addressee, enabling both of them to enter and
stay in communication.[10]

To each of these factors corresponds a different function of
language. Should a verbal act be oriented mainly towards the
referent or context, as in

(50)   John is handsome and intelligent

it would have a primarily **referential** function. Should it be focused
on the addresser and express his attitude towards what he is saying,
as in

(51)   I am getting bored talking about it

it would have an **emotive** function. Should it be centered on the
addressee, as in

(52)   Hey, you! Listen carefully!

it would have a **conative** function. A verbal act may also be aimed
primarily towards the contact; it may be used, for instance, to
check whether the channel works or to establish and prolong
communication, as in

(53)   Hello! Can you hear me?

or

(54)   Do you know what I mean?

In this case, it mainly has a **phatic** function. It may be focused on the message for its own sake and draw our attention to its sound patterns, diction, syntax, structure, etc., as in

(55)   Peter Piper picked a peck of pickled peppers;

it would then fulfill a so-called **poetic** function. Finally, it may be oriented towards the code and convey information about it, as in

(56)   'Flicks' means 'movies';

this would fulfill a **metalinguistic** function.[11]

Like any verbal act and, indeed, any signifying process, any narrative can be described in terms of similar factors. Thus, should certain parts of the narrative pertain to the narrator and his attitude towards what he is narrating ("With pain we record it, this first ecstasy was soon disturbed", *Notre-Dame de Paris*), we could say that they have an emotive function; should they concentrate on the narratee ("The reader has no doubt turned over the admirable works of Rembrandt", *Notre-Dame de Paris*), we would say that they have a conative function; and should they be focused on the code of the narrative, we could say that they primarily fulfill a metanarrative function. In other terms, the metanarrative component of a given narrative does not consist of any and all passages referring to that narrative or its constituent parts and should not be confused with the self-referential component. Rather, it is made up of those passages which explicitly refer to its code and which I call metanarrative signs.

Let us define a metanarrative sign more precisely by patterning our definition on that of a metalinguistic sign. Consider the following statements made up of linguistic signs:

(57)   Destruction is terrible
(58)   'Destruction' is terrible
(59)   Killing is bad
(60)   'Killing' is a present participle
(61)   Freshmen are always nice
(62)   'Freshmen' means first-year students

(57), (59) and (61) tell us something about the world (a certain world); more particularly, **destruction**, **killing** and **freshmen** designate certain objects or actions in that world and they, as well as the terms predicated on them, refer us to that world. On the other hand, (58), (60) and (62) do not tell us very much about the world; rather, they tell us something about words, about signs in a language. Specifically, '**destruction**', '**killing**' and '**freshmen**' do not designate anything else but the word 'destruction', the word 'killing', the word 'freshmen', and the terms predicated on them merely refer us to these words as words, to these signs as signs. (58), (60), and (62) are metalinguistic statements and the predicates in them are metalinguistic signs. In other words, a sign is metalinguistic when it is predicated on a linguistic unit taken as an element in the linguistic code.[12]

In a given narrative, there are many elements — many series of signs — which tell us something about a certain world. But there may also be elements which explicitly comment on such and such another element x in the narrative and which provide an answer to such questions as "What does x mean in the (sub-) code according to which the narrative is developed?" or "What is x in the (sub-) code used?", or again "How does x function in the (sub-) code according to which the narrative can be read?" Each one of the commenting elements constitutes a metanarrative sign: each one is a sign predicated on a narrative unit considered as an element in the narrative·code.[13]

Note that, according to this definition, a narrative passage like

(63) Shirley, who had always been very cheerful, was crying all the time

contains no metanarrative signs (though it may suggest that there is a mystery to be solved and lead to a question such as "How is it that Shirley is crying all the time?") On the other hand,

(64) Shirley, who had always been very cheerful, was crying all the time. This was a mystery

does: **this was a mystery** explicitly tells us that Shirley's behavior is a unit in the hermeneutic code framing the narrative and that it must be taken as constituting an enigma.

Furthermore, note that there may be passages in a narrative which explicitly teach us something about the conventions of the world of the narrated but which are not metanarrative. For instance,

(65) "It is the idea of duration — of earthly immortality — that gives such a mysterious interest to our own portraits. Walter and Elinor were not insensible to that feeling, and hastened to the painter's room." ("The Prophetic Pictures")

(66) "Polder behaves as though he has been placed under eternal obligation by Rickett. . . It is the same everywhere. The men who would not take the trouble to conceal from you that you are an incompetent ass . . . will work themselves to the bone in your behalf if you fall sick or into serious trouble." ("The Phantom 'Rickshaw'")

(67) Apartment dwellers always hate their neighbors and so John hated Peter

tell us something about certain laws governing certain worlds and explain certain feelings and attitudes in terms of these laws; but no part of (65)–(67) is predicated on a narrative unit taken merely as an element in the code. Instead of answering such questions as

(68) What is the meaning of unit x in the (linguistic, proairetic, hermeneutic. . .) code framing the narrative?

or

(69) What is the function of unit x in the (linguistic, proairetic, hermeneutic. . .) code framing the narrative?

parts of (65)–(67) answer something like "Why x?" (Why did Walter and Elinor hasten to the painter's room? Why does Polder act as though he has been placed under eternal obligation by Rickett? Why did John hate Peter?) Similarly, as I have indicated earlier, there may be various passages which underline the organization of the narrated or the act of narration but which do not constitute metanarrative signs. In

(70) "Our readers must have already perceived that D'Artagnan was not a common man" (*Les Trois Mousquetaires*)

and

(71) "We have just said that, on the day when the Egyptian

> and the archdeacon died, Quasimodo was not to be found
> in Notre-Dame" (*Notre-Dame de Paris*)

there is no element which explicitly answers questions like (68) or
(69).[14]

Note also that passages which implicitly or indirectly refer to
and comment on the nature, meaning or function of other passages
need not be considered metanarrative. After all, any sign in a system may be said to carry within itself an implicit comment on the
meaning (or nature, or function) of all other signs in that system
since it makes sense only in relation to them and vice versa. Indeed,
the meaning of a particular element may be arrived at not by reference to the code but by reference to the context, by an examination
of its connections with the other elements making up the sequence
within which it appears. Consider, for example, the following
passage from *The Sun Also Rises*:

> (72) "She took a telegram out of the leather wallet. . ... 'Por
> ustedes?' I looked at it. The address was: 'Barnes, Bur-
> geute'. Yes, it's for us."

Yes, it's for us is obviously an answer to **Por ustedes?** and it can be
concluded, therefore, that the latter expression means something
like **Is it for you?**. But **Yes, it's for us** cannot replace **Por ustedes?**
in the linguistic code; it is not predicated on **Por ustedes?**; and it
does not directly answer a question such as "What does **Por
ustedes?** mean in the linguistic code used?" The meaning of **Por
ustedes?** is arrived at mainly through contextual operations.

Finally, note that it is not the shape of an element but its relation to another element which makes it metalinguistic or, more
generally, metanarrative. In

(73) Jogging is funny

and

(74) 'Jogging' is funny

we find the same predicate. But, in the former,

(75) is funny

is predicated of a certain event in a certain world and refers us to
that world; whereas, in the latter, (75) is predicated of a linguistic

sign and is, therefore, metalinguistic. In the same way, identical sets of elements may function differently in different narrative passages. Given

(76)   John was handsome and he had reached adulthood
and
(77)   John had his own house, which meant that he had reached adulthood,
(78)   he had reached adulthood

functions metanarratively (metaculturally) in (77) only.

The most evident metanarrative signs – though not necessarily the most numerous or the most important – are probably those which comment on linguistic code units. A text may define an esoteric expression, a technical term, a regionalism, or even a perfectly ordinary phrase. In *Eugénie Grandet*, the narrator writes:

In Anjou, the **frippe**, a colloquial word, designates what goes with bread, from butter spread on toast – the commonest kind – to peach preserve, the most distinguished of all the **frippes**;

and in *Le Père Goriot*, several terms belonging to the jargon of thieves are explained:

Sorbonne and **tronche** are two energetic words of the thieves' vocabulary invented because these gentry were the first to feel the need of considering the human head from two standpoints. **Sorbonne** is the head of the living man, his intellect and wisdom. **Tronche** is a word of contempt, expressing the worthlessness of the head after it is cut off.

A narrator may also explain the meaning of an element in his lexicon because he is using it in a rather special way: fearing that his private diary – and, consequently, his aspirations to sainthood – may be discovered by his immediate family, the protagonist of *Journal de Salavin* decides to use 'tourist' and 'tourism' for 'saint' and 'sainthood' respectively and he informs us of his decision. Sometimes, it is a foreign word or idiom which is translated into the language of the text. In *The Sun Also Rises*, for instance, the narrator states "Afición means passion. An aficionado is one who is passionate about the bull-fights"; and in *La Chartreuse de Parme*, the narrator gives the French equivalents to many of the Italian phrases scattered in his narration. Sometimes, it is the meaning of an abbreviation which the text provides: because he finds 'tourist' and 'tourism' ridiculous and inadequate, the hero of *Journal de Salavin* chooses to use 'S.' and 'St.' instead and he announces it in his diary; moreover, referring to his work, he explains:

Since last November, I am fulfilling the functions of secretary for advertising in the offices of Icpom. This grotesque word means: Industrial Company of Pasteurized and Oxygenated Milks.

Finally, a text may define the various proper names appearing in it. In fact, this kind of definition is common even when the narrator is not particularly inclined to give explanations. Within a few pages of Flaubert's "Un Coeur simple," for example, we find: "Robelin, the farmer of Geffosses. . .Liébard, the farmer of Toucques. . .the Marquis de Gremanville, one of her uncles. . . M. Bourais, a former lawyer. . .Guyot, a poor devil employed at the town hall. . ." Note that in a passage such as

    (79)   John got up and left
there is no metalinguistic definition since the predicates refer to the person named John; however, in
    (80)   John, the shoemaker, got up and left
the *shoemaker* may be said to have a metalinguistic function since it is predicated on the sign 'John' and indicates something like
    (81)   John is the name of the shoemaker
or
    (82)   'John' means 'the shoemaker'

In many narratives, one may also find various passages referring to the non-linguistic codes subsumed under the narrative code. In such cases, the text does not comment on what a sentence, for instance, means in the linguistic system adopted; it informs us about the meanings which the signified of this sentence has in (some of) the other codes framing the narrative. If I read

    (83)   "Fabrice was so shaken up that he answered in Italian: L'ho comprato poco fa (I just bought it now)" (*La Chartreuse de Parme*)

it is the meaning of the Italian sentence in terms of a linguistic code which is given to me. But if I read

(84) She had a rifle of her own, which meant that she had fought in the war

or

(85) She was carrying a red umbrella, which meant that she was a Communist

in neither case does the text answer any questions about the linguistic nature or significance of any of the words and sentences constituting it. Rather, in both cases, the text indicates explicitly the meaning of the state of things presented in terms of a socio-cultural code; in other words, it specifically answers such questions as

(86) She had a rifle of her own. What did it mean according to the relevant sociocultural code?

and

(87) She was carrying a red umbrella. What did it mean according to the relevant sociocultural code?

Similarly, in "Sarrasine," when I read after the detailed description of a hideous old man accompanied by a ravishing young woman

(88) "Ah! it was death and lifer indeed!' "

it is not a linguistic meaning which is revealed to me but the meaning of the couple in a symbolic system. Given any narrative passage, metanarrative signs can thus indicate its functioning in a series of codes. They can explain its linguistic, sociocultural, or symbolic meaning. They can point out that a certain behavior or a certain state of things represents an enigma or a solution to that enigma: during the *petite madeleine* episode of *A la recherche du temps perdu*, Marcel underlines several times the mysterious nature of the extraordinary sensations he has; and in *Le Temps retrouvé*, a great many passages are explicitly presented as the definitive solutions to this mystery. Metanarrative signs can also show that a series of events belong to the same proairetic sequence and they can name the sequence: think of chapter and section titles which indicate at least one of the meanings of a set of activities in a narrative; or else, consider the many demonstrative + noun groups which summarize a series of sentences or paragraphs, as in

(89)   John punched Jim, then Jim kicked John, then they threw bottles at each other. This fight lasted a few seconds only

In short, metanarrative signs can illuminate any aspect of the constituent signs of a narrative.

Whether they mostly appear in the main body of a text (*Le Père Goriot, Eugénie Grandet*) or in the footnotes (*Les Bestiaires*) whether they are ostensibly introduced by a narrator or by a character (in the course of a dialogue, for instance, or in a letter sent by one character to another); whether they precede the signs they explain ("Fear, I said, that's what *miedo* means") or, as is usually the case, follow them

(I had taken six seats for all the fights. Three of them were barreras, the first row at the ring-side, and three were sobrepuertas, seats with wooden backs, half-way up the amphitheatre. *The Sun Also Rises*);

whether they are detailed and precise or, on the contrary, general and vague; whether they refer to linguistic units, hermeneutic units, or cultural ones; and whether they comment on the shape, the meaning, or the appropriateness of a given unit, metanarrative signs may fulfill several functions.

They may, for example, contribute to the rhythm of a narrative by regularly slowing the pace at which new events are presented: it is obvious that they do not so much bring new information on the narrated as they constitute an interpretation of old information. They may work as a characterization device: a character who states the symbolic meaning of an event or explains a foreign locution clearly differs from characters who never perform similar actions. They may also help define a narrator, his narratee and their relationship. In the first place, the number, the kind and the complexity of a narrator's metanarrative comments can contribute to making him pompous or unassuming, modest or conceited, cunning or straightforward, and so on and so forth. Second, the mere presence of such comments may constitute precious information on the very identity of the narratee and ultimately underline an important dimension of the narrative. In *Journal de Salavin*, the numerous metanarrative signs peppering the protagonist's diary ("Mme Baratti, the concierge. . .M. Mayer, the director of personnel, M. Amigorena, the deputy chief accountant. . . ," etc.) indicate that, far from writing for himself only, as he asserts again and again, Salavin may be writing for other readers who, he hopes, will understand him and sympathize with his plight: why else would he explain terms which he knows perfectly well? Rather than a mere private diary, it is perhaps a kind of tale which Salavin composes, a tale in which he can play the part of the hero and thanks to which the most trivial incidents in his daily life acquire importance. *Journal de Salavin* may therefore represent not only the itinerary of an unhappy consciousness in the modern world but also a meditation on the magic of telling about oneself, of narrating one's life; and it is the metanarrative component of the novel which brings this forward. Finally, metanarrative signs tend to reveal how a given narrator views the knowledge and sophistication of the audience he is addressing: the metanarrative explanations which he feels obliged to provide and the degree of tact which he manifests in providing them show what he thinks of his narratee, whether he respects him, is well disposed towards him, or considers himself to be infinitely superior; and the distribution of these explanations may point to a change in the relationship between the two: if the narrator stops making metalinguistic statements, for instance, it may be because he has understood that his narratee can do without them.[15]

But their most obvious and most important function is probably an organizational and interpretative one. Above all, metanarrative signs are glosses on various parts of a text and on the codes underlying them. To some extent at least, they point out the set of norms and constraints according to which the text deploys itself and makes sense; they present a model for its decipherment; they put forward a program for its decoding. In other words, they partially show how a given text could be understood, how it should be understood, how it wants to be understood. As I have indicated earlier, reading a narrative, understanding it, implies organizing it and interpreting it in terms of several codes. Metanarrative signs do part of this work for us. In their absence, it is up to us to determine the various connotations of a given passage, the symbolic dimensions of a given event, the hermeneutic function of a given situation, and so on. Metanarrative signs provide us with some specific connotations; they make some symbolic dimensions explicit; they define the hermeneutic status of some situations. On the one hand, then, metanarrative signs help us understand a narrative in a certain way; on the other hand, they force us (try to force us) to understand it in this way and not another. They thus constitute the answer of a text to the question: "How should we interpret you?"

Note that this is always a partial answer. We do not know of any narrative which makes the code framing it entirely and perfectly explicit, and for a very good reason: how would anyone compose a narrative in which every element or sequence of elements is accompanied by its definition and function in a variety of codes? Note too that the partial answer is not necessarily enlightening. Metanarrative signs may not come when we expect them most or they may come when we don't expect them anymore; they may never appear in passages which are quite comlex, and, on the contrary, they may abound in passages which seem to present no particular difficulties. Indeed, the explanations they supply may be trivial, redundant or tautological. In this case, their ultimate role is not so much to clarify the meaning of the specific elements they comment on but rather to underline their importance (or to minimize the significance of other elements which are not glossed). In Breton's *Nadja*, for example, there is a veritable profusion of metanarrative signs. However, they do not have a strongly explicative dimension. When the narrator writes that the word **haunt** "says much more than it means," when he states that the term **incantation** "must be taken literally," when he uses the expression **perverse objects** and adds that it must be understood "the way I understand it and like it," he does not really explain this word, this term, this expression. Rather, he provides a commentary which makes them more, not less, impenetrable. Similarly, when the narrator identifies an event as mysterious without even suggesting why, or when he reformulates one enigma — "Who am I?" — into another one which is surely more bizarre — "Whom do I haunt?" — he tends to obscure rather than illuminate the various hermeneutic terms along which his narrative is moving. Finally, when he names 'strange adventure' an explicitly strange sequence of events, he is being, at the very best, banal and redundant. Breton's metanarrative interventions do not increase our understanding of the signs to which they refer; but they certainly draw our attention to them and insist on their sign value, their sign nature. Instead of making a passage transparent, metanarrative signs in *Nadja* increase its opacity. They emphasize the sign rather than its meaning: Breton's novel, like life according to the surrealist, is full of signs and, like life, it takes on the appearance of a cryptogram.

Note also that metanarrative signs may lead us by indirection to a valid reading of a particular text. For it may happen that, instead of acting as aids to a proper decoding they constitute an obstacle to it. Put forward by an ill-informed (or ill-intentioned) narrator, or by an ignorant character, the explanations provided are sometimes incomplete — while being given as entirely satisfactory — and set the decoder on the wrong track. Sometimes also, they contradict other metanarrative comments and thus augment the difficulties of decipherment. Often, they provide totally wrong information which, if accepted, can only lead to faulty conclusions. In such cases, the reading ostensibly proposed by the text is a poor one and only by realizing it can we reach more satisfactory results.

Note finally that, if metanarrative signs guide our reading, they also help us understand better the stance taken by a narrative with regards to its own communicability and legibility as well as to the activity of reading in general. Their very presence in a text emphasizes the fact that portions of it, at least, are legible in certain ways. Their appearance is similar to that of a (fragmentary) text in the text, representing a language that is **other** in the language of the text and establishing some of the interpersonal coordinates of a communicative situation. Since they operate as decipherments of various passages and, as such, act as partial replacements for them, they help specify the assumptions of the text and the decoding contracts endorsed by it. In other words, they clarify the premises of textual communicability (if you read me according to the hermeneutic code, you will see how everything will fall into place; if you interpret me in terms of a symbolic code, you will understand that I am saying much more than I seem to; I will summarize for you this sequence of events and that one, but you will have to summarize the others). Furthermore, if reading a narrative means adding to it a metanarrative commentary, not only do they indicate what such a commentary may consist in and how it may intervene but they help specify the distance between a text's own meta-commentary and the metacommentary of a given reader. After all, both the text and the individual reader can interpret certain passages in terms of the same (sub-)codes and reach the same conclusions; but it can also happen that the text summarizes a set of activities in one way and the reader in another; or that the text finds a certain event mysterious whereas the reader does not; or that the text indicates only one symbolic aspect of a situation while the reader thinks of several others. In short, metanarrative signs tell us how we read.

THE READER

Although a text may answer many of my questions explicitly, unequivocally and correctly, there may frequently be points in my reading where, in order to find an answer, I have to rely not only on my linguistic knowledge and the textual information supplied but also on my mastery of logical operations, my familiarity with interpretive conventions and my knowledge of the world. I have already pointed out how, in the case of (37) and (38), the text provides an answer to a given question without spelling it out. Very often, however, I need much more than textual data and arithmetic or syllogistic operations to arrive at an answer. Consider the following:

(90)   John was seven foot two
(91)   Jim was throwing a big party and Mary went to the store to buy some scotch

Given (90), I am able to answer

(92)   Was John very tall?

in the affirmative because I believe that anybody over six foot five is very tall and because I know that my belief is not uncommon. As for (91), it provides explicit answers to such questions as

(93)   Who was throwing a big party?
(94)   Where did Mary go?
and
(95)   What was she going to buy?
But in order to answer
(96)   Why did Mary go buy some scotch
with something like
(97)   She went to buy some scotch because Jim was throwing a
       big party,

I not only have to assume that Jim's party and Mary's action are somehow connected but I also have to know that one often drinks scotch at parties. Reading is not, therefore, merely equivalent to the processing, through questions and answers, of semantic data explicitly provided by the text or logically implied by it.

Indeed, if it is obvious that reading depends on the text being read, it is also obvious that it depends on the reader reading that text. In the first place, and even though the questions I ask while reading are – to a certain extent, at least – constrained by the text since they must be somewhat relevant to it, we must remember that the set of possible questions is very large, especially beyond the level of individual sentences and their denotational meaning, and that I am the one who, in the final analysis, decides which questions to ask and which not to ask. Given a narrative text, for instance, I may tend to ask questions pertaining above all to the way in which some of the activities recounted combine into larger activities; or I may decide to focus on elements in the text which constitute enigmas to be solved and look for the solution to these enigmas; or else, I may attempt to find out whether certain elements in the world of the narrated function symbolically; and so on. Reading

(98)   The hunchback entered the Post Office, bought a *jeton*,
       went to the telephone and spoke for a very long time

I might wonder about the identity of the hunchback or the meaning of the term *jeton*, or I might do both, or I might ask still other questions. Depending on the questions asked, I will reach certain answers which may lead me to modify some of the information I have already gathered and which may govern, in some measure, some of the questions I will pose as I go on reading. In other words, depending on the questions asked, my reading will vary more or less considerably.

Moreover, if a text frequently allows only one correct answer to some of the questions asked, it also frequently allows more than one answer to some other questions. In fact, it may allow an indefinite number of valid answers to a given question. After all, a text may be partly constituted by words and sentences having many possible linguistic meanings, only a few of which it specifies as irrelevant (through metalinguistic commentary, for example); it may lead to a large number of inferences which are neither mutually exclusive nor mutually dependent; it may be summarizable in several ways; it may lend itself to several symbolic interpretations; and so forth. If we asked what *Journal de Salavin* was about, for instance,

(99)   It is about an unhappy consciousness in the modern world

and

(100)   It is about the magic of narrating one's life

would both constitute acceptable answers; similarly, if we asked what connotations the name Bonnelly had in *En attendant Godot*,

(101)   Bonnelly suggests **"bon et lie"**

and

(102)   Bonnelly evokes **"bon Eli"**

would both be valid enough; and if we asked how the first fifty pages of *Finnegan's Wake* could be summarized, we could come up with a very large number of perfectly suitable answers. Of course, the answers would determine, to some extent, what further questions and answers would arise and would thus affect reading. Given

(103)   Starving children can be fun and John loved fun,

if I answered

(104)   What can be fun?

with

(105)   To starve children

rather than
   (106)   Children who are starving,
I will answer
   (107)   What was John's attitude towards children?
with
   (108)   He loved to starve them
rather than
   (109)   He loved to be around starving ones

A text may thus lend itself to being read in many ways which are more or less different from one another and a reader may read that text in any of these ways.

As I have stated earlier, any reader contributes significantly to his reading of any text. First, and very generally speaking, he must be capable of perceiving visually presented symbols; he must have the capacity to store information, retrieve it and modify it as necessary; and he must possess the competence to make inferences and deductions. Just as importantly, he will make certain fundamental assumptions about the set of symbols he is deciphering. For one thing, he will assume that they are interpretable, that they do make some sense; for another, he will assume that they cohere, or can be made to cohere, into various trans-sentential patterns, even though they may seem strangely disparate at first. Finally, he must bring to his reading various kinds of knowledge and interpretetive strategies. As (90)–(97) indicate, the reader must have a certain knowledge of the world (of certain worlds) in order to answer certain questions (or even raise them). Furthermore, he must be acquainted with several codes or sub-codes. He will obviously use a linguistic code, which will allow him to understand the linguistic meaning of the words and sentences making up the text; but he may also use a symbolic code allowing him to map that linguistic meaning onto other signifying systems (sociological existential, psychoanalytic, etc.); and he may use a hermeneutic code, leading him from enigmas to solutions; a code of characters thanks to which he can organize the text around heroes, false heroes, villains, helpers, donors, or still other roles; a literary code, allowing him to recognize that the text belongs to a narrative genre – the romance, the epic, the fairy tale – and can be read in terms of the conventions of that genre; and so on.[16]

Naturally, a given reader may be very tired or not at all, very young or very old, in an excellent mood or a bad one; he may have a very good or a very deficient memory, a very large or very small capacity for decentration, a considerable or moderate attention span; he may know next to nothing or an awful lot; he may be a more or less experienced reader; he may be reading the text for the first, second, or hundredth time; he may want to read for pleasure or out of a sense of duty; he may demonstrate a particular interest in the language, the plot, the characters, or the symbolism; he may hold one set of beliefs or another; and so forth. In other words, his physiological, psychological and sociological conditioning, his predispositions, feelings and needs may vary greatly and so may his reading: his knowledge, his capacities, his interests and his goals (partly) determine the conventions and presuppositions he takes to underlie the text, the kinds of connections he is particularly eager to make, the questions he decides to ask and the answers he finds for them. In fact, the same reader may read the same text differently on different occasions.

LEGIBILITY

We often characterize a (narrative) text in terms of its readability: we say that it is highly readable, or barely readable, or practically unreadable, and we usually mean that it is more or less easy to decipher and make sense of and that it is more or less interesting and pleasing. It is clear that, just as reading a text is a function of the text and the reader, so is the readability of that text; more particularly, just as reading varies with the individual reader, so does readability. After all, one reader may find it more difficult than another to extract meaning from a particular novel because his knowledge of various codes and interpretive conventions is more limited. Similarly, one reader may find it more boring than another to read a certain story because he is less psychologically motivated to do it. It is therefore practically impossible to measure the readability of a given text. However, it is perhaps not as complicated or hopeless to try and assess at least in part what I call its legibility: the legibility of x can be equated with how easy it is to make sense out of x and that easiness can be computed in terms of the number of operations it takes to make sense, their complexity, their diversity, and their very possibility given x. In other words, to determine how legible a given text is, we would have to determine how many questions one must ask in order to arrive at certain answers, how complicated they have to be, how different they are one from the other, how they can be answered, and even whether they are answerable at all. We would thus not be concerned with whether a given reader shares the assumptions of a given text, whether he knows the conventions and codes necessary to decipher that text, whether he is experienced, or whether he is in the right frame of mind, but rather with such problems as the number of conventions and codes necessary for any reader to make sense out of that text. Of course, should we attempt to define the narrative legibility of a narrative text, we would be particularly concerned with how well the text lends itself to narratively relevant operations (ones directly related to such features as plot, chronology of events, hermeneutic units, and so on and so forth).

Consider the following:

(110)   "Apportez-moi une bière," said the man
(111)   "Bring me a beer," said the man
(112)   It was 110 degrees in the shade. "Boy! It sure is cold today!" said Joan sarcastically
(113)   It was 110 degrees in the shade. "Boy! It sure is hot day!" said Joan cordially

According to the above discussion, (110) is less legible than (111) since knowledge of two linguistic codes is needed in order to understand it; and (112) is less legible than (113) since more operations are required in order to establish what Joan meant. Similarly, we could say that a story like

(114)   John met Joan, then, as a result, John was unhappy; before John met Joan, he had been happy

is less narratively legible than one like

> (115)   John had been happy, then John met Joan, then, as a
> result, John was unhappy

since the chronological order of its events is more difficult to arrive at; and we could say that a novel like *La Bataille de Pharsale* is less narratively legible than *Eugénie Grandet* because it does not lend itself as readily to interpretation along proairetic lines, or that *Gravity's Rainbow* is less narratively legible than *Ragtime* for similar reasons.

Note that, in assessing the degree of legibility of texts, many textual features must be taken into account; so many, in fact, that I will not attempt to deal with all of them (nor could I succeed, if I attempted to!). Thus, I will not examine the influence of material criteria on legibility, although it is well known that such features of a text as the size of the symbols constituting it, their shape, or their spacing play a role in making it more or less legible. Nor will I discuss problems of style, although, once again, it is well known that such features as sentence length and sentence structure affect more or less considerably our capacity (and inclination!) to read a text. Rather, I will concentrate on certain traits which seem to me particularly pertinent to narrative texts, though often not exclusively so.[17]

The more work (per number of constituents)[18] a text requires in order to be understood, the less legible it is. All other things being equal, an ambiguous text would then be less legible than a non-ambiguous one since the processing of the information it carries would certainly prove more complicated. Similarly, a text requiring much updating of information, a text where little of what is given remains given, is less legible than one in which the given is more stable. Imagine, for example, a novel in which the name of the protagonist would change very frequently (and without any warning); or in which the same setting would be described very differently at several different points; or in which one could never be sure whether an event had occurred or not because the text would constantly send contradictory signals. In general, if the text conforms to what it has already said (if it is consistent with itself), it is more legible than if it does not. Moreover, this "principle of consistency" applies not only to the universe presented by the text but also to the way this universe is presented: a text alternating between narrative discourse and lyric poetry, for instance, is more difficult to process than one adopting narrative discourse from beginning to end; and a text written in several different languages is more difficult to interpret than one using a single language.[19] The more homogeneous a text is, the more legible it is.

If legibility decreases when the textual information is not clear (ambiguous texts) or when it is not consistent (heterogeneous or contradictory texts), it also decreases when the textual information is not sufficient or sufficiently explicit (elliptical texts, vague texts) and when it proves to be incorrect or irrelevant (deceptive texts). All other things being equal, a novel where information crucial to the understanding of a particular situation or event is not presented will be less legible than one in which all of the information needed is provided. One of the reasons why some modern narratives (and even less modern ones) are difficult to read even though they adopt such conventional forms as those of the pornographic tale or detective story is that they keep immoderately silent: the difficulties encountered in understanding exactly what is going on in Raymond Queneau's *Pierrot mon ami* partly come from the fact that it is a detective story which never names the detective, the crime committed, or the criminal; the disturbing quality of some of Bataille's fictions — *Histoire de l'oeil, Madame Edwarda, Le Mort* — results, to some extent, from the many holes in the tissue of events and situations presented; and we know how much trouble *Armance* has occasioned simply because Stendhal did not bother to mention that his protagonist was sexually impotent. Similarly, should a text supply what information is necessary but do it through implication and suggestion rather than explicit and direct statements, its legibility will be affected: to reconstruct what is zeroed, to recover what is deleted, to arrive at meaning by inference requires more operations to be performed. Given (112), for example, and in order to understand what Joan meant, I have to go through a series of questions and answers like

(116)   What was the temperature? 110 degrees.
(117)   Is that very hot? Yes.

(118)   What does Joan say? That it is very cold.
(119)   But doesn't she know that it is very hot? Of course.
(120)   What does she mean then? She is being funny and really
        means that it is very hot.

Ironic texts, allusive texts, suggestive texts may be considered elliptical and are less legible than their opposites.

The legibility of a text also depends on how deceptive that text
is, and textual deception can take many forms. Two events in a
narrative may be presented as temporally contiguous, for instance,
even though they are not: something else happened in between
which, for any number of reasons, the text did not see fit to mention at the time. Or else, a narrator may imply that a certain piece
of information is particularly important to the understanding of a
given situation, yet that piece of information proves to be totally
irrelevant. Or again, the narrator could make statements which are
supposed to be helpful and confirm or institute a degree of coherence among various events but his statements do not make any
sense: consider a narrator writing:

(121)   As we pointed out earlier, John was very much in love
        with Mary
when nothing of the sort was ever pointed out
and
(122)   As we shall see later, Joan spent the last years of her life
        traveling

when Joan's traveling is never even mentioned again. More generally, the narrator may provide all sorts of information which has
to be discarded or reinterpreted when it becomes clear that he is
far from reliable: he is a liar, he is stupid, he is insensitive, he is
not really conscious of what is going on. In short, a deceptive text,
by encouraging false assumptions and conclusions, by leading to
the wrong questions and the wrong answers, can only make for
more difficult reading.

Obviously, there are many other factors which contribute to
textual ambiguity, heterogeneity, insufficiency, or deception – and
thus to a diminution of legibility – and which are relatively easy
to isolate and describe. Should events in a narrative be textually

but not temporally contiguous or should the order of their appearance in the text not correspond to the order of their occurrence in time, more operations would be required to establish the chronology along which the narrative is deployed. It is no accident that children's stories, fairy tales, folktales and parables follow chronological order very closely; or that modern narratives – in their refusal to constitute mere objects for consumption and digestion – often favor significant disturbances in the chronology of the events they present. Like chronological disorder, spatial instability can affect legibility: events that are contiguous in the space of the text but not in that of the narrated, frequent switches of the action in space (especially when they are not explicitly indicated) can mislead and necessitate frequent readjustment and readaption. Consider

(123)   At ten o'clock, John finally kissed Mary. Peter sighed and Janet smiled

and imagine that the setting for the kiss proves to be different from the setting of the sigh and the smile. Of course, disturbances in the spatial and temporal scheme of the narrative can transcend the level of the narrated: whenever there is no clear distinction made between the here-and-now of the narration and the there-and-then of the narrated, for instance, whenever we do not know whether we are on one level or the other, as in

(124)   "I point this out now because now I was overcome by a fit of profound fitness" (*Au moment voulu*)

legibility will be seriously perturbed.

A multiplicity of points of view can have the same consequences, especially when the different points of view adopted represent different degrees of authority and reliability or, what is perhaps more disconcerting, when it is difficult or impossible to relate with certainty a given passage to a specific point of view. Similarly, even if spatio-temporal contiguity and textual contiguity correspond, and if the same point of view is maintained throughout, a narrative which generates in parallel fashion several actions around several different centers (by presenting several protagonists each with his own distinct story, for instance) will be less legible than a narrative exploring one action around one center. Finally – and this is in part a corollary of my statements about spatial, temporal or point of view perturbations – whenever a text invites a question more or less explicitly but delays providing the information necessary for answering it, the processing of textual data becomes more arduous. Thus, should a narrative introduce a character without quickly giving his name or should it open a sequence of actions but postpone closing it, its legibility is decreased.

Other serious disturbances may occur along hermeneutic lines: there are, for example, many references to an enigma but what it consists in is never made clear; or there is an enigma and there is a solution, but they are one and the same; or even, there is an answer, but we never find out what the question is. Sometimes too, serious disturbances occur in the proairetic armature. The main activities recounted (getting up in the morning, shaving, preparing for a fight, etc.) may be presented only through a mere enumeration of their component parts ("he stretched his arms, wiggled his toes, opened and closed his mouth three or four times, put his left hand over his face, etc.") and may not be immediately recognizable for what they are; or else, the activities recounted may be so heterogeneous that it is very difficult to combine them into larger activities and make them cohere into meaningful sequences: much information may be provided but it is irrelevant because it is unrelated to what textually precedes or follows it.[20]

But perhaps the most striking perturbations (and the most exploited by modern texts in general and modern narratives in particular) are the ones that take place in what we may call the referential system of the text. I have already mentioned in passing the difficulties occasioned by narratives which use many different names to designate the same character but do not make clear that they all apply to him. The reverse phenomenon can raise even more problems: imagine a narrative – or think of Faulkner's *The Sound and the Fury* or Ionesco's *La Cantatrice chauve* – in which two, three, or ten different characters all bear the same name. A character's name functions like a summary of his attributes: its stability partly guarantees the stability of the world presented and allows us to organize large segments of that world around it; should it be put in doubt or disappear, the stability of the narrative as a whole would be threatened.

Such referential problems may extend beyond characters and their names, with different nouns referring to the same object and the same noun to different objects, even though (or because!) coherence and unambiguousness would be imperiled. If I read

(125)   The blue book was thick

then, a little later and in the same context,

(126)   The blue book was beautiful

I may easily conclude that the same object is the topic of both statements, especially since thickness and beauty are not necesarily contradictory. Yet (125) and (126) may be referring to two different objects and the text could go on with

(127)   The two blue books were very interesting

Similarly, if I read

(128)   John came out of the restaurant

a few lines after a restaurant has been mentioned, I may well believe that the same restaurant is being referred to and I may be wrong. Moreover, suppose I read in a descriptive passage

(129)   The chair was comfortable

(130)   The seat was nice

and

(131)   The armchair was small

the three statements could pertain to the same object; and suppose I read

(132)   The old woman and the young woman were working hard and, although she was tired, the mother was singing

'the mother' could turn out to designate not the old woman but the young one.

Finally, certain pronominal uses may be the sources of various ambiguities or incoherences. Consider, for instance,

(133)   John put a beautiful orange in a sumptuous bowl, placed the bowl on the living-room ledge and thought that Jim would appreciate it

where the 'it' could conceivably refer to the orange, the position of the bowl or John's action; or think of such simultaneist novels as Sartre's *Le Sursis* in which identical pronouns appearing in contiguous sentences or even in the same sentence refer to different objects:

(134)   "My Führer, my Führer, you speak and I'm changed into stone, I don't think anymore, I don't want anything anymore, I am only your voice, I'd wait for him at the exit, I'd shoot him in the heart, but I am first of all the spokesman of the Germans and it is for the Germans that I have spoken, stating that I am no longer disposed to remain an inactive and calm spectator while this madman from Prague thinks he can, I will be this martyr, I did not leave for Switzerland, now I don't want to do anything but endure this martyrdom, I swear to be this martyr, I swear, I swear, I swear. . ."

Just as there are many textual factors which decrease legibility, there are, conversely, many factors which increase it by making the text homogeneous, unambiguous and easy to interpret. I have already discussed how non-deceptive metanarrative signs present a partial decoding program and, in a way, do some of our reading for us by determining explicitly the connotations of a given passage, the symbolic dimensions of an event, the meaning of a foreign expression. Besides, in many narratives, commentary which is not metanarrative may be textually prominent and function as an important guide to reading. It could be directly provided by a narrator explaining the motivations of a character, disentangling a very entangled situation, assessing the moral value of an act, or eliminating various ambiguities; or it could occur in the course of a character's meditation, or during a dialogue, or in a series of letters, and so on and so forth.[21] Along with explanations, textual justifications bring coherence to what may otherwise seem incoherent: what could be perceived as a sudden and fundamental break in a given pattern may be shown to be part of that pattern; what could be viewed as an irrelevant digression may be shown not to constitute a digression at all; what could be considered as a violation of the norms followed by the text may be justified in terms of one set of laws or another. Various organizational elements can also help insure a certain degree of legibility. Some metanarrative signs underline the proairetic and hermeneutic articulation of the text; anaphoric and epiphoric references add homogeneity and make for smooth transitions; intrusions by the narrator remind us of what has taken place, announce what will take place, and thus orient our questions or confirm our answers; and strong distinctions among characters, spatio-temporal settings and actions point to an uncomplicated model for processing and storing information. Most generally speaking, textual redundancy — at the architectural and contentual level, in the deep structure or the surface structure — is the most important ingredient of textual coherence. It may consist in (patterned) repetition of phonological and graphological features (as in rhyming and alliteration) or of semantic features (as in synonymy, near synonymy, antonymy, hyponymy, and paraphrase); it may manifest itself through frequent definitions of the terms used or periodic summaries of the material presented; it may result from the sustained use of certain rhetorical figures; and so on. Redundancy may have a more strictly narrative nature. Sometimes, the subplot in a given model parallels the plot of that novel; with the technique of *mise en abyme*, it can even reproduce it entirely on a small scale. Similarly, several plot units are repeated (the hero performs one difficult task, then another one, then another one; he violates various interdictions; he liquidates a series of lacks) or several characters perform identical or similar actions. Or else, the name of a place underlines its symbolic significance, the name of a character captures his essential qualities, the settings for his actions emphasize his deepest feelings, and so forth. Finally, if the distance between the questions raised or suggested by a text and the answers provided by that text is relatively small, legibility will tend to be relatively high. Should a character be mentioned, for instance, he is immediately introduced; should an order be given, it is quickly carried out; should a sequence of actions be opened, it is rapidly closed; should a mystery be posed, it is rapidly solved. In short, and once again, any element in a text which facilitates the processing and storing of information contributes to the legibility of that text.

Note that a text can be highly legible yet not readable, and vice versa. When discussing the notion of readability, I stated that a text is usually considered readable not merely because it is easy to decode and make sense of but also because it is interesting and pleasing. Now, a text may be so legible that it becomes unreadable. Too much homogeneity, too much redundancy too much explicitness may result in a lack of interest and a lack of pleasure. A text consisting of one sentence repeated a thousand times can be very boring; and a narrative where there is very little action and very little change, where most of what is given remains given, where there are few surprises, few mysteries and few problematic passages can become tedious very quickly.[22] Conversely, a text which abounds in ambiguities or favors discontinuity and is therefore not highly legible can be quite stimulating for that very reason. In fact, most narratives which are considered to be readable — if not most narratives — tend to strike a balance between too much legibility and too little of it. In the classical detective story, for example, the complexity of hermeneutic lines is often counteracted by the abundance of metanarrative commentary, the coherence of characterizations the strength of proairetic articulation. The distance between the fundamental question and its answer, between the enigma and its solution may be great but it is offset by the (relative) simplicity of the other problems raised. Similarly, in the so-called adventure novel, the difficulties which may arise from a complicated proairetic development are frequently compensated by the straightforward articulation of the text along other lines.

Note also that — as the above more than suggests — saying that one text is more legible than another does not necessarily mean that it is better (or worse). Legibility may be more or less valued by different people, in different cultures, for different purposes. The same can be claimed about readability; for there is no compelling reason to maintain that the interest a work evokes and the pleasure it affords constitute sound measures of its worth. Indeed, avant-garde writers have determinedly pursued the unreadable (or the minimally readable) not only by trying to un-make sense rather than make it but also by putting in question the very notion that a text should be pleasing, interesting, and entertaining.

A study of narrative taking reading into account allows us to explain why a given novel or story can be and often is interpreted in a number of ways: the proairetic dimension, like the thematic one, or the symbolic one, depends not only on textual data but also on its reader. It also provides a way of comparing texts in terms of legibility: there are complex and simple texts just as there are complex and simple sentences; there are texts which are highly legible along one axis (the proairetic one, for instance) but not another (the symbolic one); there are texts which become more legible as they deploy themselves and others which become less legible. Moreover, the description of a given text in terms of its legibility, by specifying how it accommodates some — but not all — reading conventions, how it lends itself to certain interpretative strategies while defeating others, illuminates the play of its intelligibility, its specificity, its **difference**. Besides, an examination of legibility can have historical and anthropological import: by clarifying the conditions for textual communicability, the premises in terms of which a given text can be deciphered, it can help us understand various ages and various cultures according to what they consider most legible or not legible at all. Finally, taking readers and reading into account is necessary for a description of at least some of the contextually bound factors which contribute to narrativity.

CHAPTER FIVE

Narrativity

There is widespread agreement about what constitutes a narrative and what does not. In particular, many people would agree that any representation of non-contradictory events such that at least one occurs at a time t and another at a time t_1 following time t constitutes a narrative (however trivial). According to this very general definition, not only would such texts as *Ulysses, Les Illusions perdues* or *The Confessions of Zeno* be narratives but so would the following:

(1) The water boiled then World War II started
(2) The water boiled then Mary graduated
(3) The water boiled then the wine boiled
(4) John was happy then John was unhappy
(5) John was very rich then Mary became very poor
(6) John was very rich then Mary became very rich
(7) John was very rich then he lost a lot of money
(8) John was very rich then he became very poor
(9) Joan felt very happy, then she fell in love, then, as a result, she felt very unhappy

There is also widespread agreement about the fact that different narratives have different degrees of narrativity, that some are more narrative than others, as it were, and "tell a better story". Indeed, there is even agreement about the comparative narrativity of various texts. Many readers would consider *Les Trois Mousquetaires* to have a higher degree of narrativity than *La Nausée* (though they may prefer Sartre's text to Dumas') and they would consider (8) and (9) to have a higher degree of narrativity than (1) and (2).

What is it that affects narrativity, that makes a story good as a story? It seems to me that, whatever it is, it must be related to the exploitation and underlining of features that are specific to or characteristic of narrative (as opposed to non-narrative and/or as described by narratologists from Aristotle to Barthes, Chatman and Labov). All other things being equal, for instance, a passage where signs of the narrated (referring to events) are more numerous than signs of the narrating (referring to the representation of events and its context) should have a higher degree of narrativity than a passage where the reverse is true:

(10)   John was unhappy, then he met Mary, then, as a result, he was very happy

is more narrative than

(11)   I am sitting at my desk trying to write down a story which my friend just told me. The room is hot and my pen is not very reliable but I must start. John (I like this name!) was unhappy, then he met Mary, then, as a result, he was very happy

and

(12)   "She withdrew her arm from his grasp, and slowly departed, pausing at the door, to give one long, shuddering gaze, that seemed almost to penetrate the mystery of the black veil." ("The Minister's Black Veil")

is more narrative than

(13)   "Now let such of our readers as are capable of generalizing an image and an idea, to adopt the phraseology of the present day, permit us to ask if they have formed a clear conception of the spectacle presented." (*Notre-Dame de Paris*)

simply because narrative is the recounting of events rather than the discussion of their representation. Likewise, a passage (mainly) devoted to the narrated and presenting relatively many time sequences should have more narrativity than one presenting relatively few because narrative is the recounting of events occuring at different times rather than at the same time. Consider, for example,

(14)   "Jussac, anxious to put an end to this, springing forward, aimed a terrible thrust at his adversary, but the latter

parried it and while Jussac was recovering himself, glided like a serpent beneath his blade, and passed his sword through his body." (*Les Trois Mousquetaires*)

and

(15) "He was a stout man, of about two or three-and-twenty, with an open, ingenuous countenance, a black, mild eye, and cheeks as rosy and downy as an autumn peach; his delicate mustache marked a perfectly straight line upon his upper lip." (*Les Trois Mousquetaires*)

Similarly, a narrative depicting a conflict of some kind should function better narratively than one depicting no conflict at all: characteristically, narrative represents a mediation through time between two sets of opposites. "The cat sat on the mat" is certainly not without interest but "The cat sat on the dog's mat" may be the beginning of a good story.

Yet narrativity and its sources are often much more difficult to pinpoint, describe and evaluate: is (7) more narrative than (8) or less? why? what about

(16) Joan was in good health, then she met Shirley, then she died

and

(17) Joan was in good health, then she became ill, then she died?

It seems to me that the narrativity of a given narrative is not only related to the constitutive elements of the latter and to their arrangement. It must also be related to the context in which the narrative is received and, more particularly, to its receiver (because of our situation and interests, what is highly narrative for you may not be highly narrative for me; what you find appropriate and what I find good at one time, you may find inappropriate and I bad at another time).

In order to understand better the distinctiveness of narrative, I will attempt to isolate in what follows various elements conducive to narrativity by paying attention both to the text and to the context, to aspects of the product and of its consumer. Specifically, in describing some of the features that a text should be endowed with to achieve a high degree of narrativity, I would not want to be understood as merely saying that if text x exhibits feature y it will constitute a good story (though chances are that it will). Rather, I would want to be understood as saying that if a receiver finds y in text x he will consider the latter to be narratively valuable.

EVENT DESCRIPTION

Any event or, at any rate, many events can be described in more than one way. To indicate that John did some walking, I can write

(18) John walked

but I can also write

(19) John raised his left foor two inches off the ground while swinging it forward and, displacing his centre of gravity so that the foot hit the ground, heel first, strode off on the ball of the right foot, etc.[1]

Now, it seems to me (and I am not the only one) that event descriptions such as (18) are more conducive to narrativity than (19). It is not so much that (19) is far more informative (or far less economical) than is necessary to describe a simple action. It is also that (18) conveys more clearly meaning directly related to man's engagement in the world. Characteristically, narrative presents more than temporal sequences of states and actions (involving some kind of conflict): it presents temporal sequences of states and actions that make sense in terms of a human project and/or a humanized universe.[2]

Given sets providing the same humanized information, such as

(20) He went to bed after eating

and

(21) He ate then he went to bed

or

(22) He lost the million dollars he had

and

(23) He had a million dollars then he lost it

why is it, then, that (21) and (23) seem more narrative than (20) and (22) respectively? Once again, it is a matter of description: both (21) and (23) preserve the autonomy of the conjoined events and a narrative mode of organization is more clearly perceptible when discrete states or actions are temporally related.

Indeed, an event which is individualized will contribute more to narrativity than one which is not. Narrative shies away from abstraction and thrives on concreteness. It concentrates on the particular and not the general. Rather than presenting sequences which are true of any set of circumstances, it tends to present sequences which depend on a specific set. Or, to put in differently, narrative prefers tensed statements (or their equivalent) to untensed ones: something like

(24)   Every human being dies

is fine (and may well appear in a narrative) but something like

(25)   Napoleon died in 1821

is better or, at least, more characteristic of narrative.[3]

If narrativity is a function of the discreteness and specificity of the (sequences of) events presented, it is also a function of the extent to which their occurrence is given as a fact (in a certain world) rather than a possibility or probability. The hallmark of narrative is assurance.[4] It lives in certainty: this happened then that; this happened because of that; this happened and it was related to that. Though it does not preclude hesitations or speculations – in fact, they can generate suspense, or function as signs of objectivity, or underline the quality of what did happen – and though, in its verbal form, it is hospitable to interrogative, or conjectural, or even negative sentences (something could have happened but did not; something did not happen but could have), narrative dies from sustained ignorance and indecision.[5] Consider, for instance,

(26)   Did he go to the movies? Did he then go to bed?

or

(27)   Perhaps he went to the movies and then maybe he went to bed

and compare them with

(28)   He went to the movies then he went to bed

This may explain in part why posterior narration is much more common than anterior, or hypothetical, or even simultaneous narration. With regard to narrativity, the (emphatic) past is preferable to the (possible) future, the conditional or the present: "It did happen" is more narrative than "It may happen," "It will happen" or "It would happen". This may also explain in part why such marginal narrative genres as the recipe lack narrativity; though recipes can be said to present events that would follow each other in time, there is no assurance that these events will occur. Rather than being paraphrased as

(29)   You will take two egg whites, then you will add sugar and flour to them, then you will put the whole thing in the oven, then you will get a delicious cake,

for example, a given recipe will tend to be paraphrased as

(30)   If you take two egg whites and if you add sugar and flour to them and if you put the whole thing in the oven for two hours, then you get a delicious cake.[6]

In general, when we read a text as a narrative, we try and process it as a series of assertions about events the occurrence of which is not in doubt. The easier such processing proves to be, the more readily a text suggests it and lends itself to it, the more narrativity that text will have.

WHOLENESS

Events that are equally discrete, specific and positive do not necessarily yield the same degree of narrativity. After all, (6)–(9) have a higher narrativity than (1)–(5) and a story (a sequence containing at least three narrative events) has a higher narrativity than a mere chronological arrangement of events: consider, for instance,

(31)   John was very sickly, then he ate an apple, then, as a result, he became very healthy

and
    (32)   John was very sickly, then he ate an apple, then he went
           to Germany

Narrativity also depends on the extent to which the events
presented constitute (or pertain to) a whole, a complete structure with a beginning, a middle and an end. A narrative made up
of (discrete, specific and positive) beginnings and/or ends is not
very much of a narrative. Compare, for example,

    (33)   At the beginning, he ate, then he walked, then he ran
or
    (34)   At the end, he ate, then he walked, then he ran
with
    (35)   He ate, then he walked, then he ran
or
    (36)   He was rich, then he got sick, then, as a result, he became
           poor

Similarly, a narrative where there is no continuant subject, no relationship between beginning and end, no (explanatory) description
of a change in a given situation, a narrative made up of middles, as
it were, has practically no narrativity. Consider

    (37)   John went to Germany, then Mary ate a peach, then the
           water boiled
or
    (38)   John got up, then, as a result, Mary read a book, then, as
           a result, the water boiled, then, as a result, Joan saw Peter

Narrative can do more than show that various events are related
temporally (and causally) though some narratives may merely do
that; it can also show that some events combine into larger events
(and vice versa). Temporal arrangements of states and activities do
not necessarily result in high narrativity. The latter springs, in part,
from totalizing and detotalizing events, from constructing and
deconstructing, from making sums and unmaking sums. It is no
coincidence that in French, for instance, the verb **conter** (to tell)
comes from the Latin **computare** (to calculate) and that in English,
we may use **recount** for **narrate** and **account** for **narration**.[7] Nar-

rative is usually not a simple concatenation of events in time but a hierarchical one.

Note that events that are the aggregates (or components) of other events may or may not be qualitatively different from the latter:

> (39)   He ran

is, in a way, made up of

> (40)   He ran, then he ran, then he ran;

on the other hand,

> (41)   he wrote a letter

is not made up of

> (42)   he wrote a letter, then he wrote a letter, then he wrote a letter.[8]

Whenever an event carries more information than the sum of its component events, whenever the whole is greater than the sum of its parts and different from it rather than equivalent to it, narrativity will tend to increase: narrative can show that like events may combine into like events but, more interestingly, and significantly, it can also show that (un)like events may combine into larger and different events.

Some wholes have a higher degree of narrativity than others. Why is it that (31) or

> (43)   John was very nice, then he met Mary, then, as a result, he became very nasty

is more narrative than

> (44)   John was on the bottom floor of the building, then he took the elevator, then, as a result, he was on the top floor?

One answer would be that a change in the health or the personality of the individual is less trivial than a change in his location and this, I believe, is often true. But the seeming wondrousness or significance of a series of events in no way guarantees a high degree of narrativity:

> (45)   John throttled a giant, then he slew a dragon, then he killed a whale

is not necessarily more narrative than (31) or (43); and (1), in spite of World War II, is certainly less narrative than (9). Besides, a change in location (or anything else) can be made (relatively) interesting. In fact, any (sets of) events in a narrative are wondrous or significant only in terms of that narrative and its context. Consider, for example,

(46)   John had always been on the bottom floor of the building, then one day he took the elevator, then, as a result, he was on the top floor forever.

or compare

(47)   He was standing, then there was a violent gust of wind, then, as a result, he was lying on the floor

and

(48)   He had always been standing, then there was a violent gust of wind, then, as a result, he would always be lying on the floor

(46) and (48) are more narrative than (44) and (47) respectively because they are more significant and their greater significance results from the fact that the changes described are not merely changes from one accidental state to another but rather changes from one fundamental state to another. The first state in (46) and (48) is the first state indeed; it is there from the very beginning and even before the beginning, as it were; and the last state is truly the last state and is there at the very end and even after the very end. Before John was on the bottom floor there was nothing different in his location and there could not be; after he is on the top floor, there will be nothing different either and there cannot be. We feel that matters are perfectly rounded and that no event preceding or following the sequence of events recounted can be narratively important. Narratives with a high degree of narrativity will not merely describe change and its results but fundamental changes and results. They will take us from the origin to the conclusion, from "Once upon a time" to "They lived happily ever after", from the onset of heterogeneity and difference back to homogeneity and indifference.

Note that narrative is a privileged mode of ontological commentary and has strong penchants for genesis and eschatology. Note also that narrative – like other signifying systems aspiring to autonomy and wholeness – traditionally deploys itself between common opening and closing points in human life (birth and death, infancy and old age, waking up and going to sleep) and, more generally, favors inversion: inside to outside, happiness to unhappiness, poverty to wealth, ignorance to learning, and so on and so forth. Of course, some narratives will endeavor to show that what is usually viewed as a beginning constitutes in fact an end and vice versa or that what is viewed as an inversion is very far from being one. Of course, too, in modern texts which pattern themselves after narrative in order to subvert it, autonomy defined by well-marked introductions and conclusions is refused and false starts as well as false endings abound.

The feeling of wholeness which a narrative conveys is clearly more than a matter of *terminus a quo* and *terminus ad quem*. Like the beginning and the end, the middle is important. If narrative presents changes, it also frequently accounts for them: one event or series of events is shown to modify an initial situation into a final one. Should the modifier not belong to the class of events commonly taken to effect the modification recounted or, in other words, should difficulty be experienced in comprehending the link between modifier and modified, the explanation of the change will not be acceptable or convincing and narrativity will suffer. Compare, for example,

(49) John was very rich, then he sneezed, then, as a result, he became very poor

and

(50) John was very rich, then he made bad investments, then, as a result, he became very poor

More generally, as I have already indicated or suggested several times, events that are not viewed as relevant to the middle (or the beginning, or the end), events that cannot be analyzed as meaningfully related to the change presented are narratively inert, threaten narrative coherence and impair narrativity.

THE ORIENTATION OF NARRATIVE

Narrative proceeds from one set of states or actions to another. At the beginning — in terms of time   a series of events are presented, each giving rise to a certain number of possibilities. Some of these are realized and some are not, and reading many a narrative is, in a way, wondering which will be and which will not and finding out: what can happen? what will happen? what is happening? what has happened? For instance, given at the outset

(51)   John was happy and he was rich and he was nice

one or more of the states may be modified:

(52)   John was happy and he was rich and he was nice, then he met Mary, then, as a result, he became unhappy

(53)   John was happy and he was rich and he was nice, then he met Mary, then, as a result, he became poor

(54)   John was happy and he was rich and he was nice, then he met Mary, then, as a result, he became nasty

(55)   John was happy and he was rich and he was nice, then he met Mary, then, as a result, he became unhappy and poor and nasty;

or else, it may look increasingly as if they are going to be modified, but, in the end, they are not. Similarly, given

(56)   John bought a gun

either John will use this gun or he will not; and given

(57)   John decided to go

either he will go or will change his mind or will be prevented from going.[9]

The realization of a possibility obviously depends on the existence of that possibility. I can use a gun only if I get hold of one; I can answer a telephone call only if somebody calls; I can die only if I am alive. What comes after in a narrative is therefore conditioned (to some extent) by what comes before and the end is conditioned by the beginning (although the road to that end can be full of surprises). Indeed narrative often underlines this by indicating more or less explicitly that some events (inevitably) cause some other events and narrativity is a function of the possibility of viewing one event as dependent on a preceding one:

(58)   It started to rain and John got wet

is more narrative than

(59)   It started to rain and John opened the cabinet.[10]

Note that any event can easily be made to follow any other event which it does not contradict and that dependency relationships are not essential to narrative. Should I start with

(60)   John rode off into the sunset

I could very well continue with

(61)   then a bird sang

(62)   then it started to rain

or even

(63)   then Mary became a millionaire

though not with

(64)   then he mounted his horse

On the other hand, many narratives are clearly concerned with showing how two seemingly disparate (series of) events are actually in a relation of causality, or subordination, or complementation, and they can usually do it without much difficulty. Given

(65)   John rode off into the sunset then Mary became a millionaire,

for example, I can easily establish a strong link between the two events:

(66)   John rode off into the sunset then Mary became a millionaire because she had bet everything she owned — 500,000 dollars — that he would.[11]

If one can say that the beginning of a narrative often dictates its end to some extent, one can also say that the end conditions the beginning. Thus, should a narrative be used to account for the occurrence of x at time t, its beginning — chronologically speaking — will be related to x. Besides, given an event in a narrative, its meaning partly depends on its consequences (if any). What comes after often illuminates what comes before. In

(67)   John met Mary then, as a result, he was very happy

and

(68)   John met Mary then, as a result, he was very unhappy

the significance of the meeting varies drastically; similarly, in

(69) Ellen traveled very often then, as a result, she became very rich

and

(70) Ellen traveled very often, then, as a result, she became very poor

the import of Ellen's traveling is radically different depending on the outcome.[12]

Many narratives can be viewed as teleologically determined.[13] Instead of certain events occuring because of preceding events, certain events happen because other events must happen. The means do not institute the end; the end institutes the means. In a sense, John is not happy (or unhappy) because he met Mary; he has to meet Mary because he is to be happy (or unhappy); and Ellen is not rich (or poor) because she traveled; she has to travel in order to become rich (or poor). As Gérard Genette puts it:

These **retrograde** definitions are precisely what we call the arbitrariness of narrative: not at all a lack of determination but the determination of means by ends...of causes by effects. It is this paradoxical logic of fiction which requires one to define any element, any unit of narrative by its functional character, that is to say among other things by its correlation with another unit, and to account for the first (in the order of narrative time) by the second, and so on – whence it results that the last is the one which governs all others and is governed by nothing: this is the essential locus of arbitrariness, at least in the immanence of narrative itself, for it is then easy to find for it all the psychological, historical, or esthetic determinants that we want.[14]

Narrative often displays itself in terms of an end which functions as its (partial) condition, its magnetizing force, its organizing principle. Reading a narrative is waiting for the end and the quality of that waiting is the quality of the narrative. When I come across even the most trivial statements in a narrative, I (may) feel – or know – that the triviality is only superficial and temporary because it is oriented, because it is meaningful in terms of what is to come. Narrativity is a function of that feeling and the more a novel or tale, for instance, is able to encourage it, the more narrative that novel or tale becomes.

Note that the orientation of narrative can thus be – and often is — a two-way one. Narrative moves back and forth from a beginning to an end which condition each other and this movement constitutes a very powerful motor of narrativity. Note also that since the end frequently determines the beginning at least as much as, if not more than, it is determined by it, since — from the beginning — the beginning is oriented by the (idea of the) end,[15] one could claim that the end comes at the beginning and before the beginning. In *La Nausée*, Roquentin realizes that he has tried to live his life as if it were a story and understands why it is impossible: in a story,

things happen one way and we tell about them in the opposite sense. You seem to start at the beginning. . .. And in reality you have started at the end. . . .and the story goes on in the reverse: instants have stopped piling themselves in a lighthearted way one on top of the other, they are snapped up by the end of the story which draws them and each one of them in turn draws out the preceding instant.

In order to preserve the power of a sequential arrangement of events on time (and, doubtless, for other reasons as well), teleologically structured narratives usually proceed as if they are looking for an end (as if that end had not already been reached) and they progress so as to find it and reach it. But certain texts are entirely based on the premise that the end which is to come has already come. Blanchot's *Au moment voulu*, for example, does not develop from a beginning to an end: the beginning is the end and such a development can only be illusory. It does not bring answers to the many questions it raises: these questions have already been answered. It does not satisfy our waiting (or its own): we are waiting for what has already passed. Now is then, first is last, and "Once upon a time" means "They lived happily ever after". *Au moment voulu* explores and constitutes the very paradox that narrative itself frequently is.[16]

THE POINT OF NARRATIVE

Like other signifying systems, some narratives have a point and some do not. Our language indicates it and so do our responses to particular narratives. As Labov says:

Pointless stories are met (in English) with the withering rejoinder, 'So what?' Every good narrator is continually warding off this question: when his narrative is over, it should be unthinkable for a bystander to say 'So what?' Instead, the appropriate remark would be 'He did?' or similar means of registering the reportable character of the events of the narrative.[17]

A pointless narrative has a low degree of narrativity indeed: I will not think that x is a good story if I do not see what its point as a story is.

But what determines the pointedness or pointlessness of narrative; One could say that the point of a narrative consists in the fact that distinct events are linked and made to constitute a whole, that they are totalized or detotalized into other events, that changes in a situation are described and accounted for, or that what comes before is shown to determine what comes after and to derive significance from it. Yet this is not a very satisfactory answer since there are perfectly well-formed narratives in which the proairetic and hermeneutic dimensions are not negligible and the beginning and the end condition each other but which may not have much of a point:

(71)   He bought a gun, then he went home, had a sumptuous meal, pulled down the shades, and killed himself

The representation of a series of events in time, however strongly linked they may be, does not necessarily make (enough of) a point.

Rather than being definable in terms of the constituent features of a given narrative, the point of that narrative is a function of its context. The narrative should be non-obvious and worth telling. It should represent, or illustrate, or explain, something which is unusual and problematic, something which is (made) relevant for and matters to its receiver: the illocutionary force of a narrative should be equivalent to that of a series of exclamatory (and not merely informative) assertions about events in time. Without desire on the part of the receiver and without the fulfillment of this desire, there can be no point to a narrative (just as there can be no narrative – period – without desire on the part of a sender to produce one).

This explains why the same narrative may seem pointless to some and not to others: I may want to know what happened at time *t* and why, but you may not; I may find an account of what happened very interesting and you may disagree. It also explains why senders of narrative messages often take pains to underline certain events as remarkable or important or crucial to foreground certain details rather than others, to establish a hierarchy of relevance; the receivers are then able to process or rearrange information in terms of a certain order, of a certain point.[18] It further explains why an unsolicited narrative must first of all awaken desire and it illuminates the dynamics of suspense in many a narrative which, in order to survive, delays the satisfaction of desire while maintaining desire: as soon as desire is fulfilled, the narrative must stop or accept to be pointless. Finally, it explains why narrative has been viewed as a unit of exchange and narrating as a mercantile act and why certain exemplary narratives emphasize the contract between the narrator and his narratee, the sender and his receiver (I will listen if you make it worthwhile, I will tell you a great story if you promise to be good), that contract on which the point of narrative depends: a tale for a day of survival (*Arabian Nights*), a story for a night of love (*Sarrasine*), a diary for redemption (*Le Noeud de Vipères*).[19]

The narrativity of a text depends on the extent to which that text fulfills a receiver's desire by representing oriented temporal wholes, involving some sort of conflict, made up of discrete, specific and positive events, and meaningful in terms of a human project and a humanized universe. If most of the examples I have used throughout this study are rarely given as narratives and barely – if at all – received as such, it is not because they are formally deficient: they are not. Rather, it is because they do not satisfy the conditions necessary for narrativity.

As in the case of legibility and readability, however, saying that one narrative has more narrativity than another does not necessarily mean that it is better or worse. Narrativity depends on the receiver and so does its value. Indeed, many narratives are valuable not so much qua narratives but rather for their wit, their style, their ideological content, or their psychological insight: there is much more than narrative in most narratives! Moreover, and paradoxically, saying that a text has some narrativity does not necessarily mean that it is a narrative; if certain narratives have minimal narrativity, certain non-narratives which adopt various narrative trappings for one reason or another may reach a high degree of narrativity at least in some of their parts: they set up chronological links between events, but the links prove to be illusory; they appear to be magnetized by an end, but the end does not come; they proceed with certainty, but the certainty vanishes; they establish hierarchies, but the hierarchies crumble; they seem eager to make a point, but they never do.

Although such is the case or, rather, because it is the case, the study of narrativity can illuminate not only the functioning of a given (non-) narrative but also the meaning of the narrative moment.

Conclusion

The goals of narratology are clear: to discover, describe and explain the mechanics of narrative, the elements responsible for its form and functioning. So are the results of the preceding discussion. In the first place, the study of the interaction between text and context emphasized the fact that the surface structure of a text is not quite what defines that text as a narrative. Depending on circumstances, a simple statement like "Mary ate the jam" can function as a narrative, and we all know the joke about the telephone book being a novel with too many characters and too little action. Saying that a text constitutes a narrative if and only if it is the representation of at least two events in a time sequence neither of which presupposes or entails the other is perhaps less illuminating than saying that a text constitutes a narrative if and only if it is processed as such a representation. The easier the processing proves to be, the more a text calls for it and lends itself to it, the more generally that text is recognized as a narrative.

Moreover, it was established that the great and bewildering array of possible written narratives can be accounted for with relatively few explicit rules expressible in the form of a quadripartite grammar and it was further established that degrees of legibility and narrativity depend on a set of well-defined textual and contextual factors. This is, I think, rewarding in itself for it leads from disorder to fundamental order. It is also enlightening. These rules and factors can help us define the specificity of any given narrative since this specificity is a function of the factors obtaining, the rules exploited, and the mode of their exploitation. They can help us compare, in addition, any two (sets of) narratives and institute narrative classes according to narratively pertinent features. What partly characterizes *Le Noeud de Vipères*, for instance, and distinguishes it from, say, *Manon Lescaut, Huckleberry Finn, Le Père Goriot*, or *La Modification* is that it portrays a self-conscious secondary narrator who is the protagonist, who switches narratees several times, and whose narration at first follows the events narrated but later becomes intercalated in them; and what partly distinguishes narratives of personal experience from Greco-Roman epics is that the former first describe the first event in time and the latter do not. Of course, as I have repeatedly pointed out, the results of a narratological investigation allow us to address problems which pertain not only to narrative qua narrative but also to psychology, anthropology, history, literary criticism, or esthetics. Why are flashbacks within flashbacks avoided in oral narratives? Perhaps in order that the production and reception of these narratives be facilitated. Why does Proust consistently favor iterative narration? Perhaps because he wants to describe essences. Why do I find *Madame Bovary* esthetically pleasing? Perhaps because of the way Flaubert uses scene in the midst of summary and vice versa.

Most generally, narratology gives us an insight into the principles governing systems of signs and signifying practices as well as our interpretation of them. To study the nature of all and only possible narratives, to account for their form and functioning, to examine how and why it is that we can construct them, paraphrase them, summarize them and expand them, or organize them in terms of such categories as plot, narrator, narratee, and character is to study one of the fundamental ways — and a singularly human one at that — in which we **make** sense. Ultimately, narratology can help us understand what human beings are.

Notes

NOTES TO THE INTRODUCTION

1. Roland Barthes, "An Introduction to the Structural Analysis of Narrative," *New Literary History*, VI (Winter 1975), 237.
2. The same kind of argument would apply to any tensed description of a single action and to any statement containing past-referring terms.
3. Of course, the reconstructed passages may be *pragmatically* presupposed or entailed by (15). But it is not quite the same thing.

NOTES TO CHAPTER ONE

1. They may also describe at the same time, the narratee or the narration.
2. On the subject of signs of the 'I', see Emile Benveniste, *Problèmes de linguistique générale* (Paris, 1966), pp. 223–285 and *Problèmes de linguistique générale II* (Paris, 1974), pp. 67–88; Gérard Genette, "Frontières du récit." *Communications* (8) (1966): 152–153; Roman Jakobson, *Selected Writings. II: Word and Language* (The Hague-Paris, 1971), pp. 130 ff; and Nomi Tamir, "Personal Narration and its Linguistic Foundation." *PTL* I (1976): 403–429.
3. See, for instance, Genette's "Frontières du récit," p. 162.
4. On intrusiveness, self-consciousness, reliability and distance, see Wayne C. Booth, *The Rhetoric of Fiction* (Chicago, 1961). pp. 149–165 et passim. I have not used the term 'reliable narrator' in quite the same way as Booth.
5. In any speech event, any first person always implies a second person and vice versa.
6. On the narratee and signs of the 'you', see, for example, Roland Barthes, "Introduction to the Structural Analysis of Narrative," p. 260; Gérard Genette, *Figures III* (Paris, 1972), pp. 265–276; Walker Gibson, "Authors, Speakers, Readers, and Mock readers," *College English* XI (February 1950): 265–269; Mary Ann Piwowarczyk, "The Narratee and the Situation of Enunciation: A Reconsideration of Prince's Theory," *Genre* IX (1976): 161–177; and Gerald Prince, "Introduction à l'étude du narrataire," *Poétique* (14) (1973): 178–196 and "Notes Towards a Categorization of Fictional 'Narratees,'" *Genre* IV (March 1971): 100–105.
7. I am following here, while modifying it, Wayne Booth's perspective in *The Rhetoric of Fiction*, pp. 155 ff.

8. On temporal relationships in narrative, see Gérard Genette's outstanding discussion in *Figures III*.
9. An interesting form of predictive narrative is what may be called hypothetical narrative. In this form, the narration would precede the narrated because the latter might never happen at all in any (real or fictive) world. Part of Georges Perec's *Les Choses*, for instance, is told in the conditional. More generally, hypothetical narrative may be said to occur whenever the narrator imagines what may happen in the future (but does not).
10. Strictly speaking, intercalated narration can be considered as the mere combination of a series of posterior (or anterior, or simultaneous) narrations.
11. Note that 'I says/I sez' is frequently used in oral narrative (and its written transcription).
12. A.A. Mendilow, *Time and the Novel* (London, 1952), p. 94.
13. Ramon Fernandez, *Messages* (Paris, 1962), pp. 60–61. On the narrative preterit, see Käte Hamburger, *Die Logik der Dichtung* (Stuttgart, 1968), pp. 59–72; Roman Ingarden, *Das Literarische Kunstwerk. Eine Untersuchung aus dem Grenzgebiet der Ontologie, Logik und Literaturwissenschaft* (Halle, Saale, 1931); Jean-Paul Sartre, *Situations I* (Paris, 1947): 16; and F.K. Stanzel, *Narrative Situations in the Novel: Tom Jones, Moby Dick, The Ambassadors, Ulysses* (Bloomington, 1971), Chapter I. On tense in narrative, see W.J.M. Bronzwaer, *Tense in the Novel: An Investigation of Some Potentialities of Linguistic Criticism* (Groningen, 1970) and Harald Weinrich, *Tempus, Besprochene und erzählte Welt* (Stuttgart, 1964).
14. Some traditional non-Western narratives, however, instead of starting with "Once upon a time," start with "There was a place".
15. In some written narratives, as many as four (or more) spatial categories can be explicitly referred to and differentiated: the space of the narrated; the space around the narrator narrating; the space in which his narratee is to read the events recounted; and the space in which he inscribes these events (the sheets of paper on which he writes, for example). The relationship among the four categories can, of course, be both complex and significant.
16. On the diary novel, see Gerald Prince, "The Diary Novel: Notes for the Definition of the Sub-Genre," *Neophilologus* LIX (October 1975): 477–481. Note that the medium of narration in a written narrative may be described as an oral one.
17. William Labov and Joshua Waletzky, "Narrative Analysis. Oral Versions of Personal Experience," *Essays on the Verbal and Visual Arts, Proceedings of the Annual Spring Meeting of the American Ethnological Society* (1966) 21.
18. Roland Barthes, "An Introduction to the Structural Analysis of Narrative," p. 237.
19. On the notion of presupposition, see, among many others, Oswald Ducrot's excellent *Dire et ne pas dire. Principes de sémantique linguistique* (Paris, 1972), which I follow very closely; Bas C. van Fraassen, "Presupposition, Implication and Self-Reference," *Journal of Philosophy* LXV (1968): 136–151; and George Lakoff, "Linguistics and Natural Logic" in *Semantics of Natural Language*, Donald Davidson and Gilbert Harman, eds. (Dordrecht, 1972), pp. 569–588. An earlier version of my discussion of presupposed information can be found in my "Presupposition and Narrative Strategy," *Centrum* I (1) (1973): 23–31.
20. See Oswald Ducrot, *Dire et ne pas dire*, pp. 1–24.
21. The underlining is mine.
22. On this subject, see, among others, Ann Banfield, "Narrative Style and the Grammar of Direct and Indirect Speech," *Foundations of Language* X (1973): 1–39;

Gérard Genette, *Figures III*, pp. 191-194; Pierre van den Heuvel, "Le Discours rapporté," *Neophilologus* LXII (1) (January 1978): 19-38; Marguerite Lips, *Le Style indirect libre* (Paris, 1926); Brian McHale, "Free Indirect Discourse: A Survey of Recent Accounts," *PTL* III (1978), 249-288; Norman Page, *Speech in the English Novel* (London, 1973); Günther Steinberg, *Erlebte Rede. Ihre Eigenart und ihre Formen in neuerer deutscher, französischer und englischer Erzählliteratur* (Göppingen, 1971), and Gérard Strauch, "De quelques interprétations récentes du style indirect libre," *Recherches Anglaises et Américaines* VII (1974): 40-73.

23. These traits may also appear in free indirect discourse and in "realistic" dialogue.
24. Cf. Lawrence E. Bowling, "What is the Stream of Consciousness Technique?" *PMLA* LXV (1950): 333-345; Louis Francoeur, "Le Monologue intérieur narratif (sa syntaxe, sa sémantique et sa pragmatique), *Etudes littéraires* IX (août 1976): 341-365; Melvin Friedman, *Stream of Consciousness: A Study in Literary Method* (New Haven, 1955); and Robert Humphrey, *Stream of Consciousness in the Modern Novel* (Berkeley, 1954).
25. On the Russian Formalists, see Ladislav Matejka and Krystyna Pomorska, *Readings in Russian Poetics* (Cambridge, Mass., 1971); Robert Scholes, *Structuralism in Literature. An Introduction* (New Haven and London, 1974), pp. 74-91; and Tzvetan Todorov, trans. and ed., *Théorie de la littérature* (Paris, 1965). On various types of) plot, see Norman Friedman, "Forms of the Plot," *Journal of General Education* VII (July, 1955): 241-253 and Robert Scholes and Robert Kellogg, *The Nature of Narrative* (New York, 1966), Chapter 6.
26. There have been many good studies of point of view. See, among others, Mieke Bal, "Narration et focalisation," *Poétique*, (29) (1977): 102-127; Seymour Chatman, *Story and Discourse* (Ithaca, 1978); Lubomír Doležel, *Narrative Modes in Czech Literature* (Toronto, 1973); Norman Friedman, "Point of View in Fiction: The Development of a Critical Concept," *PMLA* LXX (December 1955): 1160-1184; Gérard Genette, *Figures III*, pp. 203-224; Jean Pouillon, *Temps et roman* (Paris, 1946); Bertil Romberg, *Studies in the Narrative Technique of the First Person Novel* (Lund, 1962); Françoise van Rossum-Guyon, "Point de vue ou perspective narrative," *Poétique* (4) (1970): 476-497; Tzvetan Todorov, *Poétique* (Paris, 1973), pp. 59-64; and Boris Uspenski, *A Poetics of Composition* (Berkeley, 1973).
27. Norman Friedman, "Point of View in Fiction," p. 1171.
28. A narrator may also adopt a collective point of view (that of a "chorus" of characters, for instance, or of "public opinion") as in *1919* or *Verdun*.
29. On point of view in Sartre's fiction, see Gerald Prince, *Métaphysique et technique dans l'oeuvre romanesque de Sartre* (Genève, 1968), pp. 17-40.
30. At a movie showing or in an oral narrative performance, the duration of viewing or listening is the same for all receivers.
31. Given a series of events e_1, e_2, $e_3...e_n$ occurring at time t or at times t_1, t_2, $t_3...t_n$ respectively, we speak of ellipsis when one of the events is not mentioned.
32. Cf. Gérard Genette, *Figures III*: 128 ff. and Seymour Chatman, "Genette's Analysis of Narrative Time Relations, *L'Esprit Créateur* XIV (Winter 1974): 353-368. The term 'stretch' is Chatman's.
33. Of course, we do not usually process a text as elliptical when the possible breaks or lacunae have no consequences.
34. Cf. Gérard Genette, *Figures III*: 145-148.

NOTES TO CHAPTER TWO

1. For a similar proposal, see Gerald Prince, "Towards a Normative Criticism of the Novel," *Genre II* (1969): 8, and Charles T. Scott, "On Defining the Riddle: The Problem of a Structural Unit," *Genre II* (1969): 137. For a discussion of transforms of elementary strings, see Noam Chomsky, *Syntactic Structures* (The Hague, 1957) and, by the same author, "A Transformational Approach to Syntax" in *Proceedings of the 1958 Conference on Problems of Linguistic Analysis in English*, A.A. Hill, ed. (Austin, Texas, 1962), pp. 124–158. Note that in the course of this study and for the sake of convenience, I may represent a proposition by a sentence which is not the transform of a single elementary string.

2. From now on, I will take 'event' to mean 'event or situation'.

3. On this subject, see Ellen F. Prince, "Be-ing: A Synchronic and Diachronic Study," *Transformations and Discourse Analysis Papers* (81) (University of Pennsylvania, 1970). I am not making distinctions between states and processes, happenings and actions, etc., because such distinctions are not relevant to my discussion.

4. For a detailed discussion of exposition, see Meir Sternberg, *Expositional Modes and Temporal Ordering in Fiction* (Baltimore, 1978).

5. E.M. Forster, *Aspects of the Novel* (London, 1927), p. 130.

6. Modifications have been studied in detail by Tzvetan Todorov, who calls them 'narrative transformations.' See his *Grammaire du Décaméron* (The Hague, 1970) and "Les Transformations narratives," *Poétique* (3) (1970): 322–333.

7. Cf. Tzvetan Todorov, *Poétique*: p. 82. For another definition of sequence, see Roland Barthes, "An Introduction to the Structural Analysis of Narrative," 252 ff.

8. On the notion of character, see, among others, Sorin Alexandrescu, *Logique du personnage* (Paris, 1974); Roland Barthes, *S/Z* (Paris, 1970): 101–102; Claude Bremond, *Logique du récit* (Paris, 1973); Seymour Chatman, "On the Formalist-Structuralist Theory of Character," *Journal of Literary Semantics* (1) (1972): 57–79; E.M. Forster, *Aspects of the Novel*, pp. 69–125; Northrop Frye, *Anatomy of Criticism* (Princeton, 1957); James Garvey, "Characterization in Narrative," *Poetics* VII (1978): 63–78; Philippe Hamon, "Pour un statut sémiologique du personnage," *Littérature* (6) (1970): 86–110; W.J. Harvey, *Character and the Novel* (London, 1976); Tzvetan Todorov, *Grammaire du Décaméron*; and Michel Zeraffa, *Personne et personnage* (Paris, 1969).

9. According to the models of Propp and Greimas, more than one character may fulfill the same function (there could be three opponents and four helpers, say). Besides, the same character may fulfill more than one function (he may be both subject and receiver, or object and opponent, and so on.) Finally, not every function need be fulfilled by a character (various social forces may constitute the sender, or the object, or the opponent, and so forth). See Vladimir Propp, *Morphology of the Folktale* (Bloomington, 1958) and, by A.J. Greimas, *Sémantique structurale* (Paris, 1966), pp. 172–191; *Du Sens* (Paris, 1970), pp. 249–270; and "Les Actants, les acteurs et les figures" in Claude Chabrol, ed., *Sémiotique narrative et textuelle* (Paris, 1973), pp. 161–176.

10. Cf. Phillippe Hamon, "Qu'est-ce qu'une description?" *Poétique* (12) (1972): 465–485.

NOTES TO CHAPTER THREE

1   See, for example, Barbara Leondar, "Hatching Plots: Genesis of Storymaking" in David Perkin and Barbara Leondar, eds., *The Arts and Cognition* (Baltimore, 1976) and Peter F. Neumayer, "The Child as Storyteller: Teaching Literature through Tacit Knowledge," *College English* XXX (1969): 515–517.

2. See Vladimir Propp, *Morphology of the Folktale* and Alan Dundes, *The Morphology of North American Indian Folktales* (Helsinki, 1964).

3. On requirements for grammars, see Noam Chomsky, *Syntactic Structures* and, by the same author, "On the Notion 'Rule of Grammar'," *Proceedings of the Twelfth Symposium in Applied Mathematics* XII (1961): 6–24; "Some Methodological Remarks on Generative Grammar" *Word* XVII (1961): 219–223; "A Transformational Approach to Syntax"; *Aspects of the Theory of Syntax* (Cambridge, Mass., 1965). See also Emmon Bach, *An Introduction to Transformational Grammars* (New York, 1964) and Paul Postal, *Constituent Structure. A Study of Syntactic Description* (The Hague, 1964). On degrees of grammaticalness, see Noam Chomsky, "Some Methodological Remarks on Generative Grammar."

4. See, for instance, Claude Bremond, *Logique du récit*; Benjamin N. Colby, " A Partial Grammar of Eskimo folktales," *American Anthropologist* LXXV (1973): 645–662; Teun A. van Dijk, *Some Aspects of Text Grammars: A Study of Theoretical Linguistics and Poetics* (The Hague, 1972) and "Narrative Macro-Structures. Logical and Cognitive Foundations," *PTL* I (1976): 547–568; Lubomír Doležel, "From Motifemes to Motifs," *Poetics.* (4) (1972): 55–90; Gérard Genot *Problèmes de calcul du récit* (Université Paris X-Nanterre, CRLLI (10) (1976) and *Problèmes de calcul du récit II* (Université Paris X-Nanterre, CRLLI (12) (1977); Robert A. Georges, "Structure in Folktales: A Generative-Transformational Approach," *The Conch II* (2) (1970): 4–17; Claude Lévi-Strauss, *Anthropologie structurale* (Paris, 1958); Thomas G. Pavel, *La Syntaxe narrative des tragédies de Corneille* (Paris, 1976); Marie-Laure Ryan, "Narration, génération, transformation: *La Grande Bretèche* de Balzac," *L'Esprit Créateur* XVII (Fall, 1977): 195–210; Tzvetan Todorov, "La Grammaire du récit," *Langages* (12) (1968): 94–102 and Grammaire *du Décaméron*; Pieter Dirk van der Ven, *From Narrative Text to Narrative Structure* (Dordrecht, February, 1978). For a general discussion of the field, see Jonathan Culler, *Structuralist Poetics. Structuralism, Linguistics, and the Study of Literature* (Ithaca, 1975); William O. Hendricks, *Essays on Semiolinguistics and Verbal Art* (The Hague-Paris, 1973); Gerald Prince, "Narrative Signs and Tangents," *Diacritics* (Fall, 1974): 2–8; and Robert Scholes, *Structuralism in Literature.*

5. See, for example, Claude Chabrol, ed., *Sémiotique narrative et textuelle.* For detailed critiques of various narrative grammars, see, among others, Claude Bremond, *Logique de récit*, pp. 9–128; Bertel Nathhorst, *Formal or Structural Studies of Traditional Tales*, (Stockholm, 1969); and Marie-Laure Ryan, "Growing Texts on a Tree," *Diacritics* VII (4) (Winter 1977): 34–46.

6. This grammar is a greatly modified version of the one presented in Gerald Prince, *A Grammar of Stories* (The Hague-Paris, 1973). Because I am mainly interested in verbal (written) narrative and for the sake of convenience, the narratives I use as examples are all verbal. This does not mean that the rules I propose cannot possibly be applied to non-verbal narratives or that the concepts they express are not transferable to them.

7.   Cf. Louis Hjelmslev, "La Stratification du langage," *Word* X (1954): 163–188.
8.   No more than what I defined as a minimal story in *A Grammar of Stories*, pp. 16–37. As the structural component will show, although any story is a narrative, not any narrative is a story.
9.   In constructing my grammar, I follow Chomsky's *Syntactic Structures*, "On the Notion 'Rule of Grammar'," and "A Transformational Approach to Syntax"; Emmon Bach, *An Introduction to Transformational Grammars*; and Paul Postal, *Constituent Structures*.
10.   In my elaboration of transformational rules, I once again follow Noam Chomsky and Emmon Bach. For an excellent discussion of the use of the word transformation in narratology, see Thomas Pavel, *La Syntaxe narrative des tragédies de Corneille*, pp. 131–147. Note that one could easily account for conjoining and embedding in terms of rewrite rules. So far, however, I have been unable to account for alternation without the help of transformations. Therefore, and for the sake of consistency, I prefer to account for any complex structure with transformational rules. Besides, a bipartite structural component has the advantage of underlining the fact that many a narrative can be considered to be made up of smaller narratives.
11.   Together, the structural and logical components account for the narrated.
12.   Given a stative event A followed by an active event B, we take B to lead to a modification of A unless the text explicitly indicates otherwise. Moreover, in the absence of any other information, we will select the most plausible modification of A as the one obtaining.
13.   If ST_2, ST_3, or ST_4 are not applied, we get a narrative in which it is impossible to determine the relationship between time of narration and time of narrated.
14.   The expression component could be equivalent to a non-linguistic signifying system. Furthermore, it is quite conceivable that some such systems could not carry out all of the instructions.
15.   Recent work in text-grammar and narratology shows that the obstacle is not insuperable and that perhaps what is needed most is patience. See, for example, Teun A. van Dijk, "Philosophy of Action and Theory of Narrative," *Poetics* V (1976): 287–338; Lubomír Doležel, "Narrative Semantics," *PTL* I (1976): 129–151; Thomas G. Pavel, "'Possible Worlds' in Literary Semantics," *The Journal of Aesthetics and Art Criticism* XXXIV (1976): 165–176; and János S. Petöfi, *Vers une théorie partielle du texte* (Hamburg, 1975).

NOTES TO CHAPTER FOUR

1.   See, for instance Roland Barthes, *S/Z*; David Bleich, *Readings and Feelings; Introduction to Subjective Criticism* (Urbana, 1975); Wayne C. Booth, *The Rhetoric of Fiction*; Michel Charles, *Rhétorique de la lecture* (Paris, 1977); Jonathan Culler, *Structuralist Poetics*; Stanley Fish, "Literature in the Reader: Affective Stylistics," *New Literary History* II (1970): 123–162; Norman Holland, *5 Readers Reading* (New Haven, 1975); Wolfgang Iser, *The Implied Reader: Patterns of Communication in Prose Fiction from Bunyan to Beckett* (Baltimore, 1974); Walter J. Ong, "The Writer's Audience is Always a Fiction," *PMLA* XC (January 1975): 9–21; Michael Riffaterre, *Essais de stylistique structurale* (Paris, 1971); Walter Slatoff, *With Respect to Readers: Dimensions of Literary Response* (Ithaca, 1970). Note

that much of what I will say about reading applies to receiving and interpreting narratives which do not adopt written language as a medium.

2. See Roland Barthes, *S/Z*: 23–28 and, by the same author, "Analyse textuelle d'un conte d'Edgar Poe" in *Sémiotique narrative et textuelle*, pp. 29–54.

3. Of course, some receivers may wonder what the significance of the time or the snow is in the overall narrative strategy; but it is not the same thing.

4. On the proairetic and hermeneutic codes, see Roland Barthes, *S/Z*; Jonathan Culler, *Structuralist Poetics*, pp. 205–224; and Josué V. Harari, "The Maximum Narrative: An Introduction to Barthes' Recent Criticism," *Style* VIII (Winter 1974): 56–77.

5. The same is true of any act of verbal communication.

6. Many non-narrative messages too are susceptible of various interpretations; but not messages framed in monolithic codes (the code of traffic lights, for example).

7. Of course, psychologists may be able to tell us how much information we can process at a time and to help us clarify the notions of maximal reading.

8. See Roland Barthes, *S/Z*: 81–83.

9. See, for instance, Roland Barthes, *S/Z*: 219; William Gass, *Fiction and the Figures of Life* (New York, 1970), pp. 24–25; Tzvetan Todorov, *Poétique de la prose* (Paris, 1971), pp. 66–91.

10. Roman Jakobson, "Closing Statement: Linguistics and Poetics" in *Style and Language*, Thomas Sebeok, ed. (Cambridge, Mass, 1960). p. 353. Some scholars prefer to speak of seven factors: Dell Hymes, for example, divides *context* into *topic* and *setting*. See "The Ethnography of Speaking" in *Readings in the Sociology of Language*, Joshua A. Fishman, ed. (The Hague, 1970), pp. 110–113.

11. Cf. Roman Jakobson, "Closing Statement: Linguistics and Poetics," pp. 353–357. Of course, a verbal act may have more than one major function.

12. For a good discussion of metalinguistic statements and signs, see Josette Rey-Debove, *Etude linguistique et sémiotique des dictionnaires français contemporains* (The Hague-Paris, 1971), pp. 43–52.

13. For a similar definition, see Gerald Prince, "Ramarques sur les signes métanarratifs,: *Degrés* (11–12) (1977): e1–e10. See also Philippe Hamon, "Texte littéraire et métalangage," *Poétique* (31) (1977): 261–284 and Pierre van den Heuvel, "Le narrateur narrataire ou le narrateur lecteur de son propre discours," *Agorà* (14–15) (1977): 53–77.

14. In other words, a narrator's intrusion or an explanation does not necessarily constitute a metanarrative sign.

15. Note that all of the explanations by the narrator (including non-metanarrative ones) similarly function as indications on his relationship with his narratee. More generally, all of the explanations in any text (including non-narrative texts) provide information on the relationship between the addresser and the addressee.

16. My description of what a reader brings to a text is, of course, very incomplete.

17. On the legibility and readability of texts, see Roland Barthes, *S/Z*; Jonathan Culler, *Structuralist Poetics*; Philippe Hamon, "Un Discours constraint," *Poétique* (16) (1973): 411–445 and "Note sur le texte lisible" in *Missions et démarches de la critique. Mélanges offerts au Professeur J.A. Vier* (Rennes, 1973), pp. 827–842; Tzvetan Todorov, "Une Complication de texte: Les Illuminations," *Poétique* (34) (1978): 241–253 and "La Lecture comme consfruction," *Poétique* (24) (1975): 417–425.

18. I am leaving aside the factor of length although it is a not unimportant one.

19. A text conforming to a reality familiar to the reader – a novel full of stock characters and situations, say – is also found easier to make sense of.
20. These informational disturbances play an important role in the strategy of many absurdist texts.
21. On (reliable and unreliable) commentary, see Wayne Booth's *The Rhetoric of Fiction*, part II.
22. In a culture valuing the new, a text is not very readable on second reading unless it is relatively complex and allows for new questions to be asked (or unless we have forgotten it!)

NOTES TO CHAPTER FIVE

1. This example is taken from Jonathan Culler's *Structuralist Poetics*, p. 143.
2. Cf. Jonathan Culler, *Structuralist Poetics*, p. 143.
3. The spatio-temporal characteristics of events will thus often play a prominent role.
4. In historical narrative, which presumably recounts a series of facts from the past, ostensible signs of subjectivity are eliminated.
5. Etymologically, narrative is linked to knowledge.
6. We usually read a recipe as a program to follow and not as a story.
7. On this subject, see Jean-Pierre Faye, *Le Récit hunique* (Paris, 1967), pp. 92–93.
8. See Zeno Vendler, *Linguistics in Philosophy* (Ithaca, 1967). pp. 97–121.
9. On this subject, see in particular Claude Bremond, "Le Message narratif," *Communications* (4) (1964): 4–32 and, by the same author, *Logique du récit*.
10. Cf. Roland Barthes, "An Introduction to the Structural Analysis of Narrative," p. 248.
11. On motivation in narrative, see Gérard Genette, "Vraisemblable et motivation," *Communications* (11) (1968); 5–21. See also Boris Tomashevsky, "Thematics" in Lee F. Lemon and Marion J. Reis, eds., *Russian Formalist Criticism* (Lincoln, 1965), 61–95.
12. It is this feature of narrative which allowed Vladimir Propp to establish his *Morphology of the Folktale*: in his seminal study, Propp defined a function as "an act of dramatis personae, which is defined from the point of view of its significance for the course of action of the tale taken as a whole" (p. 20); he was able to show that the structure of Russian tales could be accounted for by thirty-one functions following an immutable sequence and whose presence or absence in a particular tale characterizes the plot of that tale.
13. The frequent occurrence in narrative of so-called narrative sentences – defined by Arthur Danto as sentences "which refer to at least two time-separated events though they only *describe* (are only *about*) the earliest event to which they refer" – is an important sign of such teleological determination. See Danto's *Analytical Philosophy of History* (Cambridge, 1965), pp. 143–181 et passim.
14. Gérard Genette, "Vraisemblable et motivation," p. 18. On beginnings and ends, see Philippe Hamon, "Clausules," *Poétique* (24) (1975): 495–526; Frank Kermode, *The Sense of an Ending. Studies in the Theory of Fiction* (New York, 1967); Youri Lotman, *La Structure du texte artistique* (Paris, 1973); Edward Said, *Begin-*

nings: Intentions and Method (New York, 1975); and Barbara H. Smith, *Poetic Closure. A Study of How Poems End* (Chicago, 1968).

15. Of course, this can take place even with narratives — *Bouvard et Pécuchet, Le Roman comique, La Vie de Marianne* — which were left unfinished.

16. *Waiting for Godot* — like *Endgame* and much of Beckett's fiction — can be viewed as presenting the dilemma of people waiting for something that is yet to come and has already gone by.

17. William Labov, *Language in the Inner City* (Philadelphis, 1972), p. 366. On the point of narrative, see also Livia Polanyi Bowditch, The Role of Redundancy in Cohesion and Evaluative Functioning in Narrative — A Grab for the Referential Hierarchy," *Rackham Literary Studies* (7) (Winter 1976): 19–35 and "Why the Whats are When: Mutually Contextualizing Realms of Narrative," *Proceedings of the Second Annual Meeting of the Berkeley Linguistics Society* (1976): 59–77; and Mary Louise Pratt, *Toward a Speech Act Theory of Literary Discourse* (Bloomington, 1977), pp. 46–47 and 132–151.

18. Frequently, of course, the sender even states, at the beginning or end of his narration, something like "The point of the story is. . ." or "What I was getting at was. . ."

19. Cf. Roland Barthes, *S/Z*: 95–96.

Bibliography

Alexandrescu, Sorin (1974). *Logique du personnage*. Tours: Mame.

Bach, Emmon (1964). *An Introduction to Transformational Grammars*. New York; Holt, Rinehart and Winston.

Bal, Mieke (1977). "Narration et focalisation." *Poétique* (29): 107–127.

Banfield, Ann (1973). "Narrative Style and the Grammar of Direct and Indirect Speech." In *Foundations of Language* X. 1–39.

Barthes, Roland (1973). "Analyse textuelle d'un conte d'Edgar Poe." In *Sémiotique narrative et textuelle*, Claude Chabrol, ed., Paris: Larousse, pp. 29–54.

– (1975). "An Introduction to the Structural Analysis of Narrative." In *New Literary History* VI (Winter): 237–272.

– (1970). *S/Z*. Paris: Seuil.

Benveniste, Emile (1966). *Problèmes de linguistique générale*. Paris: Gallimard.

– (1974). *Problèmes de linguistique générale II*. Paris: Gallimard.

Bleich, David (1975). *Readings and Feelings: Introduction to Subjective Criticism*. Urbana: National Council of Teachers of English.

Booth, Wayne C. (1961). *The Rhetoric of Fiction*. Chicago: University of Chicago Press.

Bowditch, Livia Polanyi (1976). "The Role of Redundancy in Cohesion and Evaluative Functioning in Narrative – A Grab for the Referential Hierarchy." *Rackham Literary Studies* (7) (Winter): 19–37.

– (1976). "Why the Whats are When: Mutually Contextualizing Realms of Narrative." In *Proceedings of the Second Annual Meeting of the Berkeley Linguistics Society*, pp. 59–77.

Bowling, Lawrence E. (1950). "What Is the Stream of Consciousness Technique?" *PMLA* LXV: 333–345.

Bremond, Claude (1973) *Logique du récit*. Paris: Seuil.

– (1964). "Le Message narratif." *Communications* (4): 4–32.

Bronzwaer, W.J.M. (1970). *Tense in the Novel: An Investigation of Some Potentialities of Linguistic Criticism*. Groningen: Wolters-Noordhoff.

Chabrol, Claude, ed. (1973). *Sémiotique narrative et textuelle*. Paris: Larousse.

Charles, Michel (1977). *Rhétorique de la lecture*. Paris: Seuil.

Chatman, Seymour (1972). "On the Formalist-Structuralist Theory of Character." In *Journal of Literary Semantics* (1): 57–79.

– (1974). "Genette's Analysis of Narrative Time Relations." In *L'Esprit Créateur* XIV (Winter): 353–368.

– (1978); *Story and Discourse*. Ithaca: Cornell U.P.

176   Bibliography

Chomsky, Noam (1965). *Aspects of the Theory of Syntax.* Cambridge, Mass.: M.I.T. Press.
– (1961). "On the Notion 'Rule of Grammar'." *Proceedings of the Twelfth Symposium in Applied Mathematics* XII: 6–24.
– (1961). "Some Methodological Remarks on Generative Grammar." *Word* XVII: 219–223.
– (1957). *Syntactic Structures.* The Hague: Mouton.
– (1962). "A Transformational Approach to Syntax." In *Proceedings of the 1958 Conference on Problems of Linguistic Analysis in English*, A.A. Hill, ed., Austin, Texas: University of Texas Press. pp. 124–158.
Colby, Benjamin N. (1973). "A Partial Grammar of Eskimo Folktales." In *American Anthropologist* LXXV: 645–662.
Culler, Jonathan (1975). *Structuralist Poetics. Structuralism, Linguistics, and the Study of Literature.* Ithaca: Cornel U.P.
Danto, Arthur C. (1965). *Analytical Philosophy of History.* Cambridge: Harvard U. P.
Dijk, Teun A. van. (1976). "Narrative Macro-Stuctures. Logical and Cognitive Foundations." *PTL* I: 547–568.
– (1976). "Philosophy of Action and Theory of Narrative." *Poetics* V: 287–338.
– (1972). *Some Aspects of Text Grammars: A Study in Theoretical Linguistics and Poetics.* The Hague: Mouton.
Doležel, Lubomír (1972). "From Motifemes to Motifs." *Poetics* (4): 55–90.
– (1973). *Narrative Modes in Czech Literature.* Toronto: University of Toronto Press.
– (1976). "Narrative Semantics." *PTL* I: 129–151.
Ducrot, Oswald (1972). *Dire et ne pas dire. Principes de sémantique linguistique.* Paris: Hermann.
Dundes, Alan (1964). *The Morphology of North American Indian Folktales.* Helsinki. Suomalainen Tiedeakatemia.
Faye, Jean-Pierre (1967). *Le Récit hunique.* Paris: Seuil.
Fernandez, Ramon (1926). *Messages.* Paris: Editions de la Nouvelle Revue Française.
Fish, Stanley (1970). "Literature in the Reader: Affective Stylistics." In *New Literary History* II: 123–162.
Forster, E.M. (1927). *Aspects of the Novel.* London: Edward Arnold.
Fraassen, Bas C. van (1968). "Presupposition, Implication, and Self Reference." In *Journal of Philosophy* LXV: 136–151.
Francoeur, Louis (1976). "Le Monologue intérieur narratif (sa syntaxe, sa sémantique et sa pragmatique)." In *Etudes Littéraires* IX (août): 341–365.
Friedman, Melvin (1955). *Stream of Consciousness: A Study in Literary Method.* New Haven: Yale U. P.
Friedman, Norman (1955). "Forms of the Plot." In *Journal of General Education* VIII (July): 241–253.
– (1955). "Point of View in Fiction: The Development of a Critical Concept." In *PMLA* LXX (December): 1160–1184.
Frye, Northrop (1957). *Anatomy of Criticism.* Princeton: Princeton U. P.
Garvey, James (1978). "Characterization in Narrative." *Poetics* VII: 63–78.
Gass, William (1970). *Fiction and the Figures of Life.* New York: Knopf.
Genette, Gérard (1972). *Figures III.* Paris: Seuil.
– (1966). "Frontières du récit." *Communications* (8); 152–163.
– (1968). "Vraisemblable et motivation." *Communications* (11): 5–21.

Genot, Gérard (1976). *Problèmes de calcul du récit.* CRLLI (10). Université Paris X-Nanterre.

— (1977), *Problèmes de calcul récit. II.* CRLLI (12). Université Paris X-Nanterre.

Georges, Robert A. (1970). "Structuie in Folktales· A Generative-Transformational Approach." *The Conch* II (2); 4–17.

Gibson, Walker (1950). "Authors, Speakers, Readers, and Mock Readers." *College English* XI (February): 265–269.

Greimas, A.J. (1973). Les Actants, les acteurs et les figures." In *Sémiotique narrative et textuelle,* Claude Chabrol, ed., Paris, Larousse, pp. 161–176.

— (1970). *Du Sens.* Paris: Seuil.

— (1966). *Sémantique structurale.* Paris: Larousse.

Hamburger, Käte (1968). *Die Logik der Dichtung.* Stuttgart: E. Klett.

Hamon, Philippe (1975). "Clausules." In *Poétique* (24): 495–526.

— (1973). "Un Discours contraint." In *Poétique* (16): 411–445.

— (1973). "Note sur le texte lisible." In *Missions et démarches de la critique. Mélanges offerts au Professeur J.A. Vier.* Rennes: C. Klincksieck.

— (1972). "Pour un statut sémiologique du personnage." *Littérature* (6): 86–110.

— (1973). "Qu'est-ce qu'une description?" In *Poétique* (12): 465–485.

— (1977). "Texte littéraire et métalangage." *Poétique* (31): 261–284.

Harari, Josué V. (1974). "The Maximum Narrative: An Introductive to Barthes' Recent Criticism." In *Style* VIII (Winter): 56–77.

Harvey, W.J. (1965). *Character and the Novel.* London: Chatto & Windus.

Hendricks, William O. (1973). *Essays on Semiolinguistics and Verbal Art.* The Hague: Mouton.

Heuvel, Pierre van den (1978). "Le Discours rapporté." In *Neophilologus* LXII (1): 19–38.

— (1977). "Le Narrateur narrataire ou le narrateur lecteur de son propre discours." In *Agorà* (14–15): 53–77.

Hjelmslev, Louis (1954). "La Stratification du langage." In *Word* X: 163–188.

Holland, Norman (1975). *5 Readers Reading.* New Haven: Yale U. P.

Humphrey, Robert (1954). *Stream of Consciousness in the Modern Novel.* Berkeley: University of California Press.

Hymes, Dell (1970). "The Ethnography of Speaking." In *Reading in the Sociology of Language.* Joshus A. Fishman, ed., The Hague: Mouton, pp. 99–138.

Ingarden, Roman (1931). *Das Literarische Kunstwerk. Eine Untersuchung aus dem Grenzgebiet der Ontologie, Logik und Literaturwissenschaft.* Halle, Saale: M. Niemayer.

Iser, Wolfgang (1974). *The Implied Reader: Patterns of Communication in Prose Fiction from Bunyan to Beckett.* Baltimore: Johns Hopkins U. P.

Jakobson, Roman (1960). "Closing Statement: Linguistics and Poetics." In *Style and Language.* Thomas Sebeok, ed., Cambridge, Mass.: M.I.T. Press, pp. 350–377.

Kermode, Frank (1967). *The Sense of an Ending. Studies in the Theory of Fiction.* New York: Oxford U. P.

Labov, William (1972). *Language in the Inner City.* Philadelphia: University of Pennsylvania Press.

Labov, William and Joshua Waletzky (1966). "Narrative Analysis. Oral Versions of Personal Experience." In *Essays on the Verbal and Visual Arts. Proceedings of the Annual Spring Meeting of the American Ethnological Society*: 12–44.

Lakoff, George (1972). "Linguistics and Natural Logic." In *Semantics of Natural Language.* Donald Davidson and Gilbert Harman, eds. Dordrecht: Reidel, pp. 569–588.

Leondar, Barbara (1976). "Hatching Plots: Genesis of Storymaking," In *The Arts and Cognition*. David Perkin and Barbara Leondar, eds., Baltimore: Johns Hopkins U. P.

Lévi-Strauss, Claude (1958). *Anthropologie structurale*. Paris: Plon.

Lips, Marguerite (1926). *Le Style indirect libre*. Payot.

Lotman, Iouri (1973). *La Structure du texte artistique*. Paris: Seuil.

McHale, Brian (1978). "Free Indirect Discourse: A Survey of Recent Accounts." In *PTL* III: 249–288.

Matejka, Ladislav and Krystyna Pomorska (1971). *Readings in Russian Poetics*. Cambridge, Mass.: M.I.T. Press.

Mendilow, A.A. (1952). *Time and the Novel*. London: P. Nevill.

Nathhorst, Bertel (1969). *Formal or Structural Studies of Traditional Tales*. Stockholm: Almqvist & Wiksell.

Neumayer, Peter F. (1969). "The Child as Storyteller: Teaching Literary Concepts through Tacit Knowledge." In *College English* XXX: 515–517.

Ong, Walter J. (1975). "The Writer's Audience Is Always a Fiction." In *PMLA* XC (January): 9–21.

Page, Norman (1973). *Speech in the English Novel*. London: Longman.

Pavel, Thomas G. (1976). ",Possible Worlds' in Literary Semantics." In *The Journal of Aesthetics and Art Criticism* XXXIV: 165–176.

– (1976). *La Syntaxe narrative des tragédies de Corneille*. Paris: Klincksieck.

Petöfi, Janós S. (1975). *Vers une théorie partielle du texte*. Hamburg: Buske.

Piwowarczyk, Mary Ann (1976). "The Narratee and the Situation of Enunciation: A Reconsideration of Prince's Theory." In *Genre* IX: 161–177.

Postal, Paul (1964). *Constituent Structure. A Study of Contemporary Models of Syntactic Description*. The Hague: Mouton.

Pouillon, Jean (1946). *Temps et roman*. Paris: Gallimard.

Pratt, Mary Louise (1977). *Toward a Speech Act Theory of Literary Discourse*. Bloomington: Indiana U. P.

Prince, Ellen (1970). "Be-ing: A Synchronic and Diachronic Study." In *Transformations and Discourse Analysis Papers*. (81) University of Pennsylvania.

Prince, Gerald (1975). "The Diary Novel: Notes for Definition of a Sub-Genre," In *Neophilologus* LIX: 477–481.

– (1973). *A Grammar of Stories. An Introduction*. The Hague: Mouton.

– (1973) "Introduction à l'étude du narrataire." In *Poétique* (14): 178–196.

– (1968). *Métaphysique et technique dans l'oeuvre romanesque de Sartre*. Genève: Droz.

– (1974). "Narrative Signs and Tangents." In *Diacritics* (Fall): 2–8.

– (1971). "Notes Towards a Preliminary Categorization of Fictional 'Narratees'." In *Genre* IX (March): 100–106.

– (1973). "Presupposition and Narrative Strategy." In *Centrum* I (1): 23–31.

– (1977). "Remarques sur les signes métanarratifs." In *Degrés* (11–12): e1–e10.

– (1969). "Towards a Normative Criticism of the Novel." In *Genre* II (March): 1–8.

Propp, Valdimir (1958). *Morphology of the Folktale*. Bloomington: Indiana U. P.

Rey-Debove, Josette (1971). *Etude linguistique et sémiotique des dictionnaires français contemporains*. The Hague: Mouton.

Riffaterre, Michael (1971). *Essais de stylistique structurale*. Paris: Flammarion.

Romberg, Bertil (1962). *Studies in the Narrative Technique of the First Person Novel*. Lund: Almqvist & Wiksell.

Rossum-Guyon, Françoise van (1970). "Point de vue ou perspective narrative." In *Poétique* (4): 476–497.

Ryan, Marie-Laure (1977). "Growing Texts on a Tree." In *Diacritics* VII (4) (Winter): 34–46.

– (1977). "Narrration, génération, transformation: *La Grande Bretèche* de Balzac." In *L'Esprit Créateur* XVII (Fall): 195–210

Said, Edward (1975). *Beginnings: Intention and Method*. New York: Basic Books.

Sartre, Jean-Paul (1947). *Situations I*. Paris: Gallimard.

Scholes, Robert (1974). *Structuralism in Literature: An Introduction*. New Haven and London: Yale U. P.

Scholes, Robert and Robert Kellogg (1966). *The Nature of Narrative*. New York: Oxford U. P.

Scott, Charles T. (1969). On Defining the Riddle: The Problem of a Structural Unit. In *Genre* II: 129–142.

Slatoff, Walter (1970). *With Respect to Readers: Dimensions of Literary Response*. Ithaca: Cornell U. P.

Smith, Barbara H. (1968). *Poetic Closure. A Study of How Poems End*. Chicago: University of Chicago Press.

Stanzel, F.K. (1971). *Narrative Situations in the Novel; Tom Jones, Moby Dick, The Ambassadors, Ulysses*. Bloomington: Indiana U. P.

Steinberg, Günter (1971). *Erlebte Rede. Ihre Eigenart und ihre Formen in neuerer deutscher, französischer und englischer Erzählliteratur*. 2 vols. Göppingen: A. Kümmerle.

Sternberg, Meir (1978). *Expositional Modes and Temporal Ordering in Fiction*. Baltimore: Johns Hopkins U. P.

Strauch, Gérard (1974). "De quelques interprétations récentes du style indirect libre," In *Recherches Anglaises et Américaines* VII: 40–73.

Tamir, Nomi (1976). "Personal Narration and its Linguistic Foundation." In *PTL* I: 403–429.

Todorov, Tzvetan (1978). "Une Complication de texte: Les Illuminations." In *Poétique* (34): 241–253.

– (1970). *Grammaire du Décaméron*. The Hague: Mouton.

– (1968). "La Grammaire du récit," In *Languages* (12): 94–102.

– (1975). "La Lecture comme construction." In *Poétique* (24): 417–425.

– (1970). "Les Transformations narratives." In *Poétique* (3): 322–333.

– (1973). *Poétique*. Paris: Seuil.

– (1971). *Poétique de la prose*. Paris: Seuil.

– (1965)., ed., *Théorie de la littérature*. Paris: Seuil.

Tomashevsky, Boris (1965). "Thematics." In *Russian Formalist Criticism*. Lee T. Lemon and Marion J. Reis, eds., Lincoln: University of Nebraska Press, pp. 61–95.

Uspenski, Boris (1973). *A Poetics of Composition*. Berkeley.

Ven, Pieter Dirk van der (1978). *From Narrative Text to Narrative Structure*. Dordrecht, February (1978). (Unpublished manuscript).

Vendler, Zeno (1967). *Linguistics in Philosophy*. Ithaca: Cornell U. P.

Weinrich, Harald (1964). *Tempus, Besprochene and Erzählte Welt*. Stuttgart: W. Kohlhammer.

Zeraffa, Michel (1969). *Personne et personnage*. Paris: Klinsksieck.

Subject Index

Author Index